KU-190-501

WITHDRAWN FROM STOCK

Academic Librarians and Cataloging Networks

£27-95+

**WITHDRAWN
FROM STOCK**

Coláiste Oideachais Mhuire Gan Smal
Luimneach

Academic Librarians and Cataloging Networks

VISIBILITY, QUALITY CONTROL, AND PROFESSIONAL STATUS

Ruth Hafter

CONTRIBUTIONS IN LIBRARIANSHIP AND
INFORMATION SCIENCE,
NUMBER 57

GREENWOOD PRESS
New York • Westport, Connecticut • London

144P

Colái
Mhu... ...mal
Lei.........ch
Class No. 027.7 HAF
Acc. No. 88502

Library of Congress Cataloging-in-Publication Data

Hafter, Ruth.
  Academic librarians and cataloging networks.

  (Contributions in librarianship and information
science, ISSN 0084-9243 ; no. 57)
  Bibliography: p.
  Includes index.
  1. Libraries, University and college. 2. Library
information networks. 3. Bibliographical services.
4. Cataloging, Cooperative—Data processing. I. Title.
II. Series.
Z675.U5H17 1986   027.7   85–24761
ISBN 0–313–24821–4 (lib. bdg. : alk. paper)

Copyright © 1986 by Ruth Hafter

All rights reserved. No portion of this book may be
reproduced, by any process or technique, without the
express written consent of the publisher.

Library of Congress Catalog Card Number: 85–24761
ISBN: 0–313–24821–4
ISSN: 0084–9243

First published in 1986

Greenwood Press, Inc.
88 Post Road West
Westport, Connecticut 06881

Printed in the United States of America

The paper used in this book complies with the
Permanent Paper Standard issued by the National
Information Standards Organization (Z39.48–1984).

10 9 8 7 6 5 4 3 2 1

To Ron and Samantha, beloved distractions

Contents

Acknowledgments

This research would not have been completed without the unstinting support, encouragement, and guidance of many faculty and staff members at the University of California, Berkeley. I would like to express my gratitude to all of them and most particularly to Professors Patrick Wilson, Harold Wilensky, and Robert Harlan for the intellectual excitement that they generated.

I would also like to thank my colleagues and friends at the Library School. I especially want to symbolically tip my hat and express my high regard for the work of Virginia Pratt and Thora Hutchinson from the Library School Library, exemplars of the humanistic and service ideals of the library world.

To Clara Cummins at Sonoma State University goes my warmest thanks for her friendship and my continuing awe at her ability to tame a word processor and to cope with any and all technical problems.

Finally my gratitude and thanks to Kate, Joyce, Katherine, and Zenobia—the best volunteer support group anyone could wish for.

Academic Librarians and Cataloging Networks

Introduction

Networks and Their Impact on Libraries

One of the most important developments affecting library and information agencies in the past decade has been the growing reliance by individual libraries on the services of automated, cooperative international networks, also known as bibliographic utilities. These utilities offer a range of products designed to help libraries exploit the fact that work done at one institution can often be utilized by another library with little or no change being required. The reason that this is possible is that library participants in a network have traditionally conformed to agreed-upon professional codes and standards of performance, and they are now willing to add network rules to their pantheon of required standards. These network rules provide, in effect, the structure for the data base management systems that make it possible for libraries to add records to, and search, the indexed files of the bibliographic utilities. Thus standards for describing the physical form and subject content of acquired material (cataloging rules) are linked to the computer software that organizes the machine-readable data in the central computer of the network system (network rules) in order to provide integrated codes for the creation of network bibliographic files.

Although network activity affects almost every aspect of library work—acquisitions, circulation, reference, etc.—its most dominant impact has always been on cataloging. Indeed, this is the first service area that the major utilities developed and it remains the most important aspect of their work. There's a simple and compelling reason why this has occurred.

The catalog is the most valuable and unique resource of each library. Traditionally this central bibliographic file has always been the focal point for all library processing activities. Catalogers create this file by following extremely complex and sometimes ambiguous codes in order to describe and classify each item added to the collection. Since adherence to the codes is a mandated professional requirement, catalogers everywhere are theoretically able to use each others' work. Therefore, development of a huge online catalog, accessible by telecommunications to all member institutions, and containing all cataloging work created by individual libraries, should result in a vast overall saving of catalogers' time without the dilution of quality inherent in most mass production activities.

This assumption is based upon several premises which the library professional literature appears to accept as given truths:

1. Cataloging created at one library can generally be utilized by most other libraries with little or no changes required.

2. Most catalogers do conform to, and correctly interpret, complex cataloging codes.

3. It is relatively simple to identify and label substandard cataloging.

4. Library administrators support catalog quality control activities.

5. Technology now makes it possible to lower cataloging costs while maintaining the quality of the bibliographic records being produced.

6. Creation of nationwide online catalogs provides benefits for catalogers, library administrators, and network personnel by positively enhancing their power and status.

On the face of it, this wonderful array of benefits seems almost too good to be believed. And, in fact, as an administrator working in a network-affiliated library, I found it hard to agree that the development of bibliographic networks was an unmixed blessing or that network participation inevitably enhanced the power and status of library and information professionals. Within my own library I found evidence of trends negatively affecting the professional status of catalogers. I also personally experienced some limitations on my autonomy as a manager as it became increasingly necessary to adapt library work schedules and cataloging standards to mandated network requirements.

As a result of these changes, I felt a need to examine the other side of the cost-benefit equation of communal data-base creation in general, and of network quality control activities in particular. After all, if that data base does save cataloging time, doesn't it also threaten catalogers' autonomy and raise the spectre of deprofessionalization of catalogers' work? Doesn't communal enforcement of quality standards create the need for peer review groups composed of cataloging experts? Are these groups more critical and less tolerant of deviation from cataloging codes than in-house supervisors? Doesn't an increased insistence on standardization and/or quality control affect the power of in-house administrators as well as increase their costs? Are the activities of network personnel influenced by standards of their customers and by the catalogers that create the network records? Are there clear-cut winners and losers resulting from the development of networks and the quality control procedures they require? Who bears the burden of technological change?

It became clear to me that any attempt to answer these questions inevitably must concern itself with the issue of the heightened visibility of work produced. Creation of network computerized files means that an immense public cataloging record is visible nationwide on every participating library's terminal. Because cataloging departments and/or their individual catalogers attach identifying codes to these records, it is possible for peers, managers, critics and consultants to evaluate their successes and failures. Once they do so, they become participants in a nationwide process of evaluation of cataloging work. This remarkable increase in the groups concerned with evaluating an individual library's product has received little attention in the library research literature and yet my own experience shows that knowledge of, and participation in, work being evaluated nationwide tends to dilute the power of in-house managers and catalogers.

As I reviewed the research literature dealing with the effect of networks on libraries I was struck by the fact that so many articles dealt solely in theories without much attempt to validate conclusions through analysis of actual changes in library or network activities. At the same time, there did exist an almost equal number of articles of the "how we loved the network and integrated with it in Library X" school of writing. What seemed to be missing and needed by the library profession was research examining comparative changes in actual library and network practice and how the new realities of library performance, standards, and evaluation practice impacted prevailing theories and beliefs about the work of library and information professionals and their management of technological change. The 1983–84 case study that I describe in this book was my response to this perceived need.

Research Hypothesis and Methodology

The research that I've outlined in this book was undertaken to provide data about the impact of new technologies and the organizations that develop them (networks) on a traditional profession (librarians in general, and catalogers in particular). In part it was done to validate my own perception of the professional changes emanating from the network-cataloger relationship. Therefore my research hypothesis was framed to provide some focus for examining negative as well as positive consequences of that relationship.

Research Problem

Library participation in bibliographic networks enhances the visibility of catalogers' work and thereby creates new processes for evaluating both the work and the status of professional catalogers. Increased reliance on computerized networks leads to

1. Increased deprofessionalization of cataloging.
2. Deflection of standard-setting authority from professional catalogers to library administrators and network personnel (quality con-

trol of cataloging becomes the foundation of social control of catalogers).

3. Enhanced activity by, and emphasis on, cataloging peer groups and less attachment to cataloging departments by professional catalogers.

4. Competing standards and techniques for quality control by catalogers, administrators, and network personnel.

Methodology

In my view analysis of issues such as work quality and organizational authority does not readily lend itself to mail questionnaires. Emotions, personal and peer group values, educational background, work history, and work environment intimately affect individual judgments about the results of introducing changes into the workplace. Thus, I made an early decision to base my research on in-depth interviews with affected catalogers, administrators and network personnel. Sixty-eight interviews ranging from one to five hours in duration took place between April 1983 and January 1984 at six libraries.

Within the libraries, the persons selected for interviews included at least 25 percent of the professional catalogers, some library assistants, the head of the cataloging department, and at least one high level administrator (i.e. Head of Technical Services, Assistant Library Director, Library Director). Some catalogers were interviewed individually and some in groups. The decision whether to interview one person or several at one time was based on the number of catalogers available for interviewing and the time constraints imposed by the host library. At networks, all directors or supervisors of quality control activities were interviewed and discussions were held with several other administrators. (The interview schedule used for the library and network discussions appears in Appendix A.) It must be noted, however, that many of these talks ranged beyond the initial questions posed in the interview schedule since interviewees were encouraged to voice their frank views about cataloging issues in their work environments. Persons interviewed were promised that they would not be directly cited for remarks they made and that is the practice followed in this report. However, relevant remarks made by interviewees in any published format, or unpublished comments that they have specifically approved, are cited.

Six academic libraries were chosen as the site for most of these interviews. Academic libraries usually require very complete bibliographic records for use by their patrons, many of whom are actively engaged in research. Another requirement for these libraries was that they belong to a cataloging network. Since each network has asserted claims about the quality of the records in its data base, libraries were also chosen to represent participation in the three major American networks (Online Computer Library Center [OCLC], Research Library Information Network [RLIN], and Washington Library Network [WLN]) in order to determine whether cataloging practitioners were significantly affected by variation in network quality control standards and practices. By happenstance, two of the six participating libraries used two of the networks, thus increasing opportunities for comparison. Of the six libraries, three participate solely in OCLC, one participates solely in RLIN, one participates in RLIN and OCLC, and one participates in WLN and OCLC. The preponderance of OCLC reflects its greater number of customers and the fact that it is used by approximately half of all academic libraries (OCLC. Users Council, 1982). The six academic libraries include three major research libraries (Stanford, Berkeley, University of Washington) and three institutions supporting academic programs up to and including the Master's degree (San Francisco State University, San Jose State University, Sonoma State University).

Libraries of middle to large size were selected using the criterion of a budget over 1 million dollars. The size criterion was imposed because smaller libraries usually do not have large cataloging departments and so cannot provide a cataloging sample that one could generalize from, or quote without danger of improperly identifying one's source.

Finally, geographic and financial considerations limited my research to a sample group located on the West Coast of the United States. However, since librarianship is an occupation characterized by national norms, national networks, and national job markets, this regional sample should still reflect current American practice.

An unanticipated source of interviews and information was the 1982 Oglebay Institute on Quality Control. During the course of my preparatory research, I was informed of, and invited to, a conference on quality control being organized by the Pittsburgh Regional Library Center. (The Pittsburgh Regional Library Center is a regional network affiliated with OCLC.) This conference, the first of its kind, was organized to review, evaluate, and critique network quality control activities. Invited participants included network personnel and catalogers who had regional and national reputations for developing and enforcing cataloging quality control standards. During the course of this conference I was able to interview many of these participants, concentrating my efforts on network designated master catalogers (e.g. participants in network advisory groups). I have included the interview material developed during that conference, plus the information published in the Oglebay Institute on Quality Control *Proceedings* (1982), in the findings discussed in this document.

In short, this study has been designed to explore influences on and experiences of information workers involved in newly computerized cataloging work environments. It is not meant to form the basis for statistical models of present-day cataloging. Moreover, no claim is made that the interview data present a comprehensive picture of American cataloging quality control programs and their side effects. Nevertheless, the number of interviews held (68) and the multiplicity of libraries and networks represented do provide a basis for tentative generalizations about the impact of technological change on the evaluation and control of the work of professional catalogers.

When evaluating these generalizations, please remember that they are linked to a specific time period which is already past history and a configuration of technology that is rapidly changing. This means, to put it bluntly, that some of the material contained in this book is already outdated. What should remain current and (I hope) of some interest to a reader is the need to continually examine library "motherhood" concepts (e.g. cataloging quality control is an unmitigated good) to determine if they ever did, or still do, provide reliable guideposts for management of the library profession.

CHAPTER *I*

Cataloging and the Network Environment

Cataloging as a Process and an Art

For more than a century librarians have debated whether a
library catalog is primarily a list designed to physically locate
material on the shelves of the library or a bibliographic tool
created to organize and explicate the bibliographic relationships existing between individual items in a library's collection
(Verona, 1959). The finding-list approach limits catalog use to
identifying and locating items that the patron is already aware
of and whose title page information he/she either remembers
or has noted as a bibliographic citation. Creating such lists is
comparatively simple and inexpensive because almost all the
information that the cataloger is seeking can be located on the
title page or some other location of the material in hand.

Finding-lists, however, are often inadequate for bringing together all the works by a given author, or all the editions of a
given work. Therefore, if a reader is looking for Mark Twain's
Huckleberry Finn, the finding tool will probably list the author's name, inverted (Twain, Mark), and the title. The fact
that Twain is a pseudonym for Samuel Clemens, and that Clemens wrote some material using his real name, would not usually be noted in the finding list nor would much cataloger effort
be devoted to organizing all Twain's production under one heading. Moreover, in such a list, various translations of *Huckleberry Finn* would be scattered under the names of the translators
or the translated title, adaptations of the book to various for-

mats (screenplay, record, etc.) would also be diffused throughout the catalog under adapters' names or new titles, and editions of the book might be located in various parts of the catalog if editors significantly changed the wording of the title from the original edition's title page. (Cataloging convention makes the title page the authoritative source of bibliographic information.) Thus, with a finding-list, an author's works, if they have been published under different names or translated titles, will not be in one cohesive file. Instead, they will be scattered throughout the catalog. As Schoenung notes (1981:54), "The product of entries created in such a manner is clearly an inventory, not a bibliographical catalog."

The focus of the bibliographic catalog is not on the physical item acquired by the library, but on its intellectual content and its relationships with other material in the library's collection. For instance, Shakespeare published his plays with variant spellings of his name and, over time, those plays have been published anonymously, in numerous formats, in many critical editions, and in translations in over 100 languages. The bibliographic catalog is developed by the cataloger to bring together all works of an author, all the editions of his/her work, and all the criticism of that work, and to provide the patron with guides to find other material that is related to that work in some way. This is primarily accomplished by using cross references ("see" and "see also" notes within the catalog that tie together material whose intellectual links would not be apparent simply by recording information from the title page), added entries (additional access points [indexing terms] for locating information about a work, such as the name of an important illustrator of one edition), and subject headings (using one or more subject terms from an authoritative list like the Library of Congress subject Headings [LCSH] to organize files within the catalog of works that are linked together by the subject they discuss) and authority files (library lists that tell the cataloger the official names that all works of an author, or forms of a title, or index entries for a subject are listed under in the bibliographic file, plus the cross references already placed in the catalog to guide patrons to the official catalog form of the name or subject).

The bibliographic catalog is far more complex and expensive

than the finding list. Although almost all librarians accept the idea that catalogs must provide multiple ways of finding any specific item that a patron is seeking (e.g. listing by author, title, and subject), libraries vary greatly in their commitment to complete bibliographic cataloging and often create hybrid catalogs that combine elements of the finding tool and the bibliographic catalog. All catalogs serve as inventories to collections, but there are great differences, even among research libraries, in the effort expended to collate the works of an author or to provide in-depth subject description of that author's work. Historically, in the United States, much greater emphasis is placed on organizing all the works of an author in one file under an official form of his/her name than in relating editions of a work to each other (Verona, 1959:84–86). Even the Library of Congress only uses some of the rules designed to bring editions of a work together and usually places limits on the number of subject headings and added entries for a work by developing criteria related to language of origin, format, or other physical or intellectual attributes.

Not only do libraries vary in the amount of information they use to catalog a book, but over time cataloging rules and procedures change. The catalog reflects shifting and dynamic intellectual concepts and relationships. Subject headings that were adequate for one period of time may need to be changed or divided to fully index the concept in the modern terminology that the patron uses when searching for information about a subject area. Rules for assigning official names to authors or titles, for dealing with subtitles, for describing multimedia materials, are revised to reflect research and theory about how information is best organized, indexed, and displayed. Within individual libraries, changing audiences for the library's catalog may affect the depth of its cataloging. Several great universities, for instance, have evolved from their original purpose as teachers' training institutes. The scope and complexity of their collections, and the catalogs that describe their content, have thus changed greatly over time. And technology also plays a role in altering cataloging codes and work procedures. The cost, time, and techniques for filing and searching for information are different in a card, microfiche, or online catalog and these considerations greatly influence library decisions about material to be included for description by the cataloger. Finally, local considerations (e.g. the size of a file to be changed when a rule is revised), budgets (what resources and personnel can be devoted to cataloging), prestige (is this the catalog of record of a research library or the less complex file of the rural branch of a public library), and research (studies about information searches) have specific effects on individual libraries and administrators at any one point in time. Of course, both the effects and the administrators will change over time and cataloging standards in the individual library will reflect those changes.

Catalogers need to learn many codes and procedures other than the present official cataloging codes and subject headings in order to describe a newly acquired item for a bibliographic catalog. They must also be aware of past cataloging practices, be able to maintain files for authoritative forms of names and titles, and know their catalog well enough to make judgments about the references required to link one file to another. All these activities and decisions must be undertaken in the context of the compromise that each library has developed between the prevailing codes and rules and its own historical practices. Therefore an acceptable cataloging entry for one library might prove totally unsuitable for another and, even more significantly, might not even be acceptable to the originating library at some later period in time.

This problem of change over time and diverse interpretation of the rules by various libraries becomes enormously magnified in a network data base. Thousands of libraries are entering records from their own unique catalogs. While most of these records have been created using Library of Congress codes, they may also incorporate local rules designed to highlight authors or collections of special interest, or to bypass Library of Congress code revisions that administrators decided were too expensive to implement. Then too, libraries vary in the rigor of their standards for cataloging work produced. As David R. Dowell notes (Krieger, 1976:174) some catalog departments were formerly considered to be "... an employer of last resort—a quiet haven for those unable to make it in other areas of the library and/or academic world." Work in these "havens" often resulted in improper interpretation of codes, in failure to update authority files, or simply in sloppy transcription of title page information onto the catalog record. As a result, substandard and variant records inevitably became part of the network data base. Other libraries seeking to use these records must now determine if variations from the cataloging codes or practice they follow are minor enough to permit full acceptance of the cataloging located in the data base, or if the cataloging copy can be edited to meet their requirements, or if the cataloging in the data base is simply unacceptable. When this latter decision is taken, libraries often originate new cataloging and input it into the data base. This means that more than one record now exists for the same item and that subsequent library users will have to choose between them or perhaps decide that both are flawed and add yet another record to the data base. Thus, without consensus on the codes that catalogers must follow when adding records to the network data base, the number of duplicate records for the same item could conceivably form a very high percentage of the automated data bases of the bibliographic utilities.

In the 1970's when computer-based network cataloging was introduced, OCLC became a virtual computerized cataloging monopoly. The major reasons for its acceptance were the beliefs that it would reduce both cataloging costs and the time required to process acquired material. Another reason for OCLC's popularity with libraries was the fact that it did not demand or enforce standardization in cataloging practice upon its users. Instead, it stressed cooperative activity in building the data base by adding as many records to it as possible and made its inputting standards loose and flexible. It was only after 1978, when other competitors began to make significant inroads upon OCLC's library market by stressing the quality of the records in their data bases, that OCLC seriously began to enforce quality control procedures. The other networks, noting the marketing advantage that a "clean" data base gave them (i.e. a data base conforming to modern codes, to Library of Congress approved forms of names and titles, and coded to organize information in the official machine readable format, MARC), became even more rigid in their standards and in their demands for conformity in the inputting of records.

One may well ask why enforcing quality control standards and conformity attracted library customers in the late 1970's when it had repelled them just years before. The answer is that just a few years of experience searching a data base had produced evidence that checking duplicate records for the same item was a costly process. Instead of training a clerk to be able to accept or adapt the one record in the data base that best described a book, cataloging staff often found three or four records that varied in the name of the main author (e.g. some libraries cataloged under the real name of the author, some under the pseudonym, some under anglicized spelling of foreign names, etc.), or in the description of the physical characteristics of the book, or in the subject headings, or in the call number for the book. In addition, some libraries continued to think of the cataloging record only as a finding tool, and thus provided minimal cataloging of the new items added to their collections. This meant that many institutions chose not to provide subject headings and/or complete physical descriptions of the items they had acquired. Deciding whether or not to use this available minimal level cataloging and/or determining which of several duplicate records best reflected the description and content of a library's recent acquisition often required the judgment of professional catalogers, thus increasing the costs of network participation through the consumption of large amounts of professional time. In other words, distinct extra costs were apparent to library administrators from the lack of quality control and consistency in the network files.

This problem continues to worry all the networks, but is of particular concern to OCLC because it possesses the largest data base (almost 11 million records as of June 1984 [OCLC 1983/84 Annual Report]) and the greatest and most varied number of customers (over 5000 participants by the end of 1983—[OCLC 1983/84 Annual Report]). Moreover, once a data base becomes large enough it provides a foundation for a multiplicity of information-based activities other than cataloging (interlibrary loan, bibliographic research, creation of union catalogs, etc.). But these new activities presume that libraries are able to find the one authoritative record in the network data base that best describes the material they are interested in. If the record does not contain enough information, or if there are competing records in the data base, the participating library cannot cheaply and easily use the new network services. The one exception to this rule is RLIN. Its development of clusters of records relating to the same item is discussed in greater detail in a later section of this chapter.

Although specific programs may vary, all networks have responded in some way to the demands for conformity and quality control voiced by their customers and demanded by the cataloging advisory groups they themselves have formed. It should also be noted, however, that they have begun to urge their patrons to automatically accept records found in the data base and not try to change each record to meet local standards of quality. They have continually emphasized that librarians need to become more flexible and search for alternative ways that an item might have been cataloged before inputting a new, and potentially duplicate, record into the communal data base.

Carol Wilson, of the Serials Control Unit of OCLC, reflects this network stance (Oglebay, 1983:9):

I have a set phrase that I use, that comes up, especially with serials catalogers, talking about "born again" catalogers, catalogers who know the one true way to catalog this serial. And not only do they want to change the online record to look like that, but they might not search any other way they know is not the one true way. Obviously that causes problems for everybody.

What really causes problems for everybody is that there is no one true way. There is a code of cataloging rules (Anglo-American Cataloging Rules 2 [AACR2]) but those rules have changed over time. There is a standardized set of subject headings (LCSH), but every month the Library of Congress makes changes, additions, and deletions to that list. There are very rigid rules created by the Library of Congress for producing a machine-readable record and for inputting it into a computerized data base (MARC), but those rules are also subject to revision. There is the de facto national cataloging copy produced by the Library of Congress catalogers, but several studies (e.g. Boissonas, 1979) show that it is inconsistent and subject to "pipeline problems" (by the time that the cataloging copy is processed through the Library of Congress bureaucracy the rules or subject headings have changed and the record is in conflict with the rules then being enforced). There is also the history of the individual library and its processing practices, the audience it serves, and the resources available to it. Any of these factors may cause a library's administrators to decree that catalogers should not spend money changing headings or providing a full physical description of an item, or, alternatively, that they should spend time adding local information to the cataloging record or extra subject headings for material of special interest to their patrons.

There is also the problem that networks differ in their coding practices. What this means is that although all networks theoretically subscribe to the same cataloging rules, they place various items in the cataloging record in different computer fields. They also provide different software and search keys and each network has developed its own codes for storing, retrieving, and manipulating information in its data base.

The inescapable fact is that developing a cataloging record often requires judgment and subject knowledge and/or competence in foreign languages, plus perspective on how the item acquired is best linked to the other material that the library possesses. The cataloger is describing the content as well as the physical appearance of the material under review. Such work is an intellectual act and is based on the presumption that the cataloger possesses the expert knowledge about the item required to be able to adequately describe it and provide access points (subject heading, title, author, call number) which will allow the vast majority of users to determine whether this material will be helpful to them and to locate it within the library. Catalogers can often differ about the best headings to describe the content of the work (e.g. should the work *Social Change in Tribal Society* be listed under "Anthropology," "Sociology," "Political Science," "Ethnology," or all four?). Their records may legitimately vary in other ways (e.g. providing contents notes or detailed descriptions of illustrations) depending upon the specialist groups and educational levels included as users of their libraries' catalogs. Thus, although computerized cataloging networks can provide copies of cataloging records created in other libraries, they have no way of guaranteeing that the records in the system suitably describe any item for all subsequent libraries that try to use them. As one cataloger has noted (Morita, 1983:1):

Intellectual content deals with the assignment of call numbers, content designators, subject headings, and other notes based on catalogers' analysis of the content and their interpretation and application of such tools as the classification schedule and LCSH. Quality control of the intellectual content of catalog records is essentially dependent on human resources. It cannot be done by machine, even with a fairly advanced online system.

It appears that the professional cataloger has only limited control over many elements in his work and yet is accountable for making those elements balance. At the same time, automation creates so many new situations for the cataloger to cope with that his/her old standards become quickly outdated. Commenting upon this seemingly endless cycle, Charles Martell, a library administrator, noted that the recent revision of the cataloging code was a product of the catalogers' frantic search for order in an environment becoming ever more disordered (Martell, 1981:5):

Code making appears to have become a continuous process. Each completed cycle results in a published code. Almost immediately a new code begins.

An epigram from Goethe's *Faust* seems applicable: "What you have received as a legacy from your fathers, you must win for yourself in order to make your own"...It appears from the perspective of this observer that there must be an inherent rightness about code revision. The authors of catalog codes seem to carry within them a desire to achieve a sense of order in a bibliographic world that is often chaotic.

But the chaos is increasing and so the codes have come faster and faster. It took 41 years, from 1908–1949, for the American Library Association and Library of Congress *Joint Code* to be revised. It is anticipated that the *Anglo American Code* second edition will last only about six years (Martell, 1981:6).

Thus, accelerating change, conflict, ambiguity, the multiplicity of standards, and the need to make judgments characterize cataloging work in the automated network environment and make it difficult to apply agreed-upon evaluation standards to the records being created by the professional cataloger.

The Network Cataloging Environment: Change Agents Enforcing Standards for Consistency

Network Description

Less than 100 years ago each library created its own bibliographic records and selected from a variety of cataloging codes the one most suited to its needs. In 1898, the Library of Congress reorganized and developed its own new rules. By 1901, it began to sell copies of its cataloging on 3 × 5 cards. As these cards gained in popularity, libraries began to use Library of Congress cataloging instead of creating their own. Library of Congress cataloging practice became increasingly accepted as the standard for bibliographic records that could be accepted nationwide. Hagler and Simmons note (1982:270–271):

In filling a vacuum and becoming the de facto leader of the English-speaking world in the techniques of bibliographic control, the Library of Congress gave practical meaning to what has become the first law of cataloging administration: "Never create a bibliographic record for a document if you can more cheaply acquire and use a satisfactory record originating elsewhere."

In 1969, the Library of Congress added an option to its card service. Customers could also receive shipments of its new bibliographic records in machine-readable format (MARC) on magnetic tape. In order to take advantage of this option, however, they would need access to expensive computer machinery, would have to develop complex software to manipulate this tape, and would need to begin hiring new kinds of library employees such as systems analysts and programming personnel.

The expenses involved in adjusting to the computer format were very high and many libraries concluded that the most reasonable way to adapt to these changes was to form consortia or networks of libraries to share development costs and to promote programs for the creation of a communal data base. Within a relatively short time these networks, utilizing a centralized machine-readable bibliographic data base which is cooperatively created by many libraries, have become "... a basic tool of librarianship" (Hagler and Simmons, 1982:277). OCLC, RLG/RLIN and WLN are the three major American networks.

OCLC

OCLC, the Online Computer Library Center, was founded in 1967 to provide cataloging support services (primarily the production of catalog cards) to a consortium of Ohio colleges. It quickly developed other services and soon expanded its market from Ohio to every state in the United States and to many other countries. It is the largest American network. Although approximately half of its 5000 customers are academic libraries, OCLC still has the most varied customer base and includes public libraries and information agencies other than libraries (e.g. research laboratories, publishing houses). By the end of June 1984, its data base contained almost 11 million records. Only 20 percent of those records came from the Library of Congress. The remaining 80 percent of the data base consisted of records input by the network's participating members. The network is governed by a Board of Trustees. A Users' Council, elected by the participating institutions, elects some trustees and also acts as an advisory committee to the board. Other important advisory groups include the Cataloging Advisory Council (CAC) and the Network Advisory Group. This latter group represents the 18 regional networks that act as brokers for OCLC services and provide the basic mechanism through which OCLC responds to customer demands.

RLG/RLIN

The Research Libraries Group was created in 1974 by four large research libraries. In 1978 RLG acquired Stanford University's bibliographic data system, then called BALLOTS. This subsequently was converted into the Research Libraries Information Network (RLIN), which is RLG's wholly owned bibliographic network. RLG operates through a Board of Governors elected by each full member institution participating in the network. RLIN's membership has expanded beyond its original four members to a 125–member national constituency and some nonacademic library participants. However, its core constituency remains the major academic research libraries. The data base contains more than 12 million records. Programming for the RLIN data base includes a particularly powerful subject-searching program which can combine subject terms and exploit the unusual richness, detail, and variety of the records created by these major research institutions.

WLN

The Washington Library Network began as a project of the Washington State Library and is the only major network that is strongly linked to a government agency. Unlike OCLC and RLIN, WLN is a regional network and its members are libraries located in Western states. WLN is national in scope, however, because its software has been purchased by libraries in several regions in the United States and in Canada. This software is highly regarded because of its online linkage of authority files to bibliographic records. WLN has the smallest data base of the three bibliographic utilities (2.5 million records). Its members include many small libraries and relatively few large academic libraries. For this reason, the composition of its data base is almost exactly the opposite of OCLC's—80 percent of its records come from the Library of Congress and only 20 percent are contributed by the network's members.

The networks vary greatly in history, size, composition, governance, and financial resources. None of them, however, would be able to operate unless participating members agreed to input records created in accordance with the Library of Congress approved cataloging code (AACR2) and its cataloging practice, and input in a standardized machine-readable format (MARC). Thus all networks require adherence to standardized rules, codes, and processes and they all have developed quality control procedures to insure that their bibliographic records conform to these standards. In effect, these procedures are designed to produce an evaluation of member-input records in order to identify catalogers and/or cataloging departments that deviate from network rules and to take appropriate measures to bring them into compliance. For this reason network-initiated quality control procedures can have a significant impact upon the evaluation of, and work standards for, catalogers in thousands of participating libraries.

Quality Control

Because many of the quality control activities of the networks are quite similar, I've found it possible to develop some generalizations about the procedures developed to monitor and enforce work standards. Where, however, networks differ significantly, variations in policy and practice are noted.

According to James Schoenung (1981, Chapter 3–4: 33–67), who has written one of the definitive studies on the quality of OCLC records, the versatility of the shared cataloging data base is the prime reason why libraries have shifted from the manual to the online system. The most important functions of the online system are

1. Searching an extremely large data base and locating bibliographic records about material in a variety of formats.

2. Cataloging books and producing bibliographic records in a variety of formats (online, cards, microfiche, etc.).

3. Inputting original cataloging when no record can be located in the data base.

4. Using the system to reclassify and recatalog older records.

5. Formatting spine and book labels and producing those labels by sending production orders to printers located at the local libraries.

6. Creating an archival tape which produces permanent machine-readable records of the library's cataloging activity.

7. Creating monthly, quarterly, or annual lists of the library's acquired materials.

8. Correcting, expanding, updating, and deleting local library cataloging.

9. Producing nationwide, standardized cooperative cataloging so that all libraries benefit from the original cataloging effort of any one member.

The equipment used by the local libraries is a custom-designed CRT terminal for displaying records, a keyboard used by the terminal operator to search, correct, and send commands to the central computer, and telecommunications equipment (modem and channel interface) to permit messages to be sent to and from the network.

When a library wants to catalog a specific item, the terminal operator keys in a unique bibliographic identifier (e.g. an International Standard Book Number (ISBN), or the Library of Congress Card Number (LCCN), or a unique search key derived from some combination of author and title. If a "hit" occurs (and it does so 80–98 percent of the time, depending upon the type of library and the network being accessed), the system responds by displaying records on the computer screen.

The terminal operator (who might be either a clerk, a library assistant, or a cataloger) compares the network bibliographic record to the item being cataloged and makes necessary corrections, additions, and deletions to the cataloging provided by the network. When this process is completed to the satisfaction of the local library, the terminal operator sends a command to the network to record the approved cataloging onto magnetic tape.

Each day the network merges the individual library's "profile" with the cataloging done by it that day in order to establish the format for the catalog card, to develop the bibliographic data to be included in various indexes, to provide material for the archive tape of the library's cataloging work, and to produce and mail the catalog cards.

When the terminal operator is unable to locate a matching record in the network data base, he/she will utilize previously established departmental rules in order to choose one of the three options:

1. Store the material for a period of time and then check the data base again to see if a suitable bibliographic record is presently available.

2. Catalog the item and input a new record into the data base.

3. Locate Library of Congress cataloging printed in the *National Union Catalog* and transcribe and enter this material into the data base.

If options 2 or 3 are chosen, then new cataloging expands the data base. Although the Library of Congress eventually catalogs most current English language material, demands of libraries (especially academic libraries) are so numerous and so varied in nature that it would be impossible for the national library ever to come close to creating all required American bibliographic records. Indeed, in all the networks the contributed copy by network participants and their addition of cataloging for unique, rare, locally interesting and/or ephemeral material is what makes the network data base far more productive than any previous tool for cooperative cataloging.

Once an item is cataloged, the library's holding symbol is added to the bibliographic record in the network data base. Within OCLC, libraries using the record can edit it to reflect their own local practices but the first record into the system (usually referred to as the "master record") remains unchanged and is the only cataloging copy available to all future searchers unless Library of Congress MARC records are received. These then "bump" the master record and become the standard cataloging copy in the data-base files.

In OCLC the practice is followed of only displaying the master record and suppressing all other records even if they have been edited to the point where local changes have substantially altered the record. This means that libraries who have edited a record are unable to see their own local cataloging displayed on the screen at any time after they have finished the editing process. They will, however, receive catalog cards and archival tapes that reflect all their local corrections.

Despite this, the OCLC data base contains many duplicate records entered under variant forms of the name of the author or title, or mistakenly entered into the file as another edition of a work when it is merely a reprint of an earlier edition. Duplicates also sometimes occur when catalogers have to make judgments about the official name of an institution. Prior to AACR2, the name of a subordinate body of an institution be-

came a subheading of that institution. Under the original Anglo-American Cataloging Rules, works created by Widener Library were cataloged "Harvard University. Widener Library."
Now AACR2 states that if the name of the subordinate body
is distinctive enough to be approached in isolation from the
name of the parent body, then the heading goes under the
subordinate's name. In this case then, the new entry would be
"Widener Library." This would be a clear-cut change of heading
except for the fact that the new rules also contain an exception—if the name of the subordinate body contains some element of dependency on the name of the higher body, the name
of the higher body becomes the main heading. In this example,
the Widener Library is very well known and its name is distinctive enough for most catalogers to make it the main entry,
but what about the Green Library at Stanford or the Doe Library at Berkeley? Obviously catalogers could legitimately differ about what form of the name to use, and the result would
be that some libraries might catalog Doe Library publications
under "Charles Frances Doe Library" and some under "University of California. Berkeley. Doe Library."

In the RLG/RLIN network, in particular, the concept of the
master record is substantially weakened. Records are set up in
clusters. If the cataloging produced by the local library does
not correspond in every detail to the record already in the data
base, it starts a new cluster. If the cataloging of the inputting
library does correspond in every major data element to some
catalog cluster, then its holding symbol is linked to the record
for that cluster. Records are then ranked in the data base to
show if they are using the official Library of Congress form of
a name or title, have completed all required data fields (see
Appendix C for definitions of computer fields), and correspond
to AACR2. Normally the Library of Congress would be the first
record in the first cluster, but if the LC record is only Cataloging
in Process (a form of preliminary cataloging utilized by the
Library of Congress), then it will be in a lower-ranked cluster.
At RLIN this cluster process is felt to be particularly valuable
to the large research libraries because it provides access to
finely detailed bibliographic records which can be utilized to
provide in-depth cataloging for researchers.

The Washington Library Network has a much stronger concept of the master record. In this network, even Library of Congress copy is subject to machine and manual revision in order to get each record to conform precisely to network-defined cataloging rules and authority files. If Library of Congress copy is sent to the network after a record that meets all network checks has already been entered, the network copy remains the master copy and is not automatically bumped by Library of Congress cataloging.

During the interviews I held with WLN staff, LC was ranked as "... one of the great polluters of the data base." The three and one half WLN cataloging revisers, who (with one exception) are professional catalogers, therefore do not place as heavy an emphasis on using LC copy as the data-base standard. The revisers study AACR2, check authority files, and make a judgment about which record stays in the file as the network master. Thus at WLN, the revisers, assisted by the computer, apply one set of standards to all records. Given this situation, it is hard to disagree with the assertion of that network's Bibliographic Maintenance Manager that "If quality is consistency, then WLN is a quality network."

In general, then, some idea of a "master record" or "master cluster" prevails in network programming. Libraries want to quickly locate an acceptable standardized record and incorporate it, with minimal or no revision, into their catalogs. This is by far the fastest and most economical way to operate because it allows clerks, rather than catalogers, to use standardized rules and procedures to make decisions about accepting cataloging copy. In fact, a study by a major academic library showed that savings of up to 20 percent of total processing costs could result from the administrative decision to accept with minimal or no changes the cataloging found by searching the network data base (Druschel, 1981).

If, however, a defective or substandard record is input into the data base, it must be reedited each time it is used by another library. Such action has many negative consequences for the network:

1. It increases the amount of time each library requires to manipulate or edit a record without a compensating increase in revenues. Li-

88502

braries pay fees based upon the number of records they use, not on the amount of time spent searching or editing the data base. If it takes more time to work on a substandard or totally wrong record, less network time will be available to search for and print good network copy. Moreover, since the number of terminals that can directly interact with the computer file at any point is far less than all OCLC terminals, heavy use of computer time by some libraries creates the effect of a constant busy signal for other libraries seeking to access the network.

2. It increases the overall number of records in the data base. Often libraries make the decision that the cataloging located, especially if it has not been produced by LC, does not describe the material they have acquired (e.g the subtitle varies slightly) and so they input a new master record. This means that expensive computer storage space for the individual record, and for all the indexes linked to it, is unnecessarily consumed by these extra records and that more expensive and complex machinery must be acquired by the network in order to accommodate the increasing number of records.

3. More records increase the complexity of the software programs because they require development of indexes to quickly link search terms to the individual records. Networks must increase their computer and personnel costs in order to develop this software.

4. It reduces potential revenue for the networks. All networks provide financial incentives to libraries inputting new records. The networks understand and support the concept that libraries incur extra costs in cataloging and inputting an original record and that the whole network benefits from their efforts. Besides, the financial credit given the original library is usually quickly amortized by the costs assigned to the other libraries that copy this record. The more libraries using an individual record, especially one where cataloging is of such good quality that the need for local editing is largely eliminated, the more profitable that record becomes. If two or three records relate to the same bibliographic item, then they dilute the per unit profit for that item and, at the same time, increase the storage and editing costs of the network.

Thus, from the point of view of the networks, substandard and/or duplicate records negatively affect costs and place unnecessary drains upon manpower and equipment resources. For these reasons, Fred Kilgour, founder of OCLC, described the quality of the OCLC data base as "Public Enemy Number 1" (Interview in Schoenung, 1981: 10).

But what constitutes substandard cataloging? In some instances it is very easy to identify. The bibliographic record, for instance, may have typographical errors that make it difficult or impossible for searchers to locate it in the data base. The author's name may be misspelled, or a key word left out of a title, or numbers transposed. On top of these typographical errors is another layer of substandard record—one supposedly input at the full cataloging standard but lacking adequate descriptive information in one or more of the required data elements (e.g. author, title, date). These are errors of omission resulting in less than a full cataloging record and requiring substantial editing by other network data-base users. There is also the type of error, resulting from professional interpretation of ambiguous cataloging rules, where two libraries, both endowed with high quality cataloging departments, decide to catalog the same book in very different ways. Then too, just as in every profession, there simply are some sloppy or poorly trained catalogers who create obviously flawed records. Finally, there are libraries that complete every subfield, add notes, and fill the library card with enormous amounts of extra information, especially if the item in hand has been acquired for a special or local collection. In one sense these libraries should be commended for scholarly cataloging and the completeness of the record. But, in another sense, these libraries have developed records that provide too much detail, are nonstandardized, and require editing by network participants. These might be termed errors of commission because they result from overzealous observance of both national and local cataloging conventions.

Whatever the cause of the error, the mere identification of it poses a threat to the status and security of the professional cataloger. If the error is typographical, then the supervising cataloger is at fault for not developing enough quality control checks to insure that library assistants and clerks have verified the material in hand before entering the record at the network terminal. If the error is judgmental, then the cataloger is being told that he/she is not properly interpreting the rules, although expertise at rule definition is the claim to professional status by the cataloger. If the error results from an overelaborate record, or one that adheres to local library rules, then the creator of that record may be held responsible for producing unnecessary extra work for all other libraries in the network.

The most obvious and most concerned evaluators are the network administrators because poor cataloging has a direct impact on the increased costs and decreased viability of the data base services they offer. All the networks recognize this problem and have created departments or sections to monitor, control, and correct errors.

Before an error can be detected, it must first be defined. In Schoenung's thesis on the quality of OCLC member input records, he defined an error as a variation by a member input record "... from cataloging data for the same records distributed by LC, as well as their conformity to OCLC input standards" (1981:xx).

OCLC has created a far more complex variety of quality control standards and procedures than Schoenung uses. That network's administrators have always sought to create programs that would help achieve a balance between the network's need and desire for a high-quality standardized data base and its users' desires to keep input costs at the lowest possible level. OCLC therefore follows two key guidelines (Ohio College Library Center, 1972):

1. Library of Congress cataloging and practices of that institution that are codified or apparent from analysis of the records being produced.

2. AACR2 when LC cataloging is not available.

These guidelines have not always resulted in standardized cataloging because the Library of Congress is not always consistent, AACR2 is often ambiguous, and sometimes the two standards (code and practice) clash directly with each other. Moreover, over the years, MARC, a standardized record format developed by the Library of Congress for the communication and exchange of machine-readable bibliographic data, has constantly been expanded and revised.

Hagler and Simmons note that AACR2 was created by a

large international committee, most MARC standards are maintained by large national committees, and LC subject headings are developed on an ad hoc basis by the personnel of the Subject Cataloging Division of the Library of Congress. Therefore "... large and numerous committees, each attacking particular detailed problems at different times and looking for compromise solutions are inherently incapable of weaving an entirely consistent fabric of standards" (1982:287).

In 1977, *OCLC Technical Bulletin* Number 30 was issued. It completely superseded earlier network input standards. It created two distinct levels of cataloging (Ohio College Library Center, 1977):

1. Level I—Full Cataloging. This is the desired level for libraries and should be used whenever possible.

2. Level K—Minimal Cataloging. This is based on the Library of Congress minimal standard which requires no name authority work. Certain descriptive elements also become optional for this level of cataloging. It was hoped that lower requirements would encourage more libraries, especially smaller libraries, to input records about unique material that they held. These records could later be upgraded to meet full standards.

In this way network policy makers developed a compromise between the need to maintain standards and the equally urgent requirements of attracting additional patrons and revenue.

About the same time, OCLC began to develop software for online error detection. The system has been designed to reject incorrect subfield codes, books whose publication date is in the future (e.g. 1986 or later, as of 1985), or improper codes in subfields. But at OCLC automatic error detection has as yet only functioned to identify the simplest errors. At WLN, by contrast, the use of the computer to check errors is far more advanced. This is because its linked online authority and bibliographic files make it possible for the computer to automatically check parts of the record as they are input at the terminal and to highlight on the CRT any data element conflicting with the authority files.

Because OCLC lacks these linked files, its major procedure

for controlling errors in OCLC is off-line error reporting to its Bibliographic Maintenance Section (BMS). The primary responsibility of this section is the quality of the records input into the cooperative cataloging data base. The section has network authorization to change any record in the online union catalog. Each month BMS reports on the corrections, changes, and deletions that it makes to records, the error reports that it has received, and how the activity compares to the year before. In 1982 alone, BMS received 48,000 Change Request Forms. These forms record errors identified by member libraries with accompanying evidence to prove that the inputting was incorrect (Oglebay, 1983:39–64).

As of 1983, BMS employed 10 staff members—five professional librarians (catalogers and systems analysts) and five paraprofessionals. These paraprofessionals process and correct 93 percent of the Change Request Forms using rules and evidentiary guidelines established by the BMS professionals in order to determine whether the record is in error (Oglebay, 1983: 41). In other words, paraprofessionals are evaluating the work of professionals, assigning errors, and correcting their work.

Some of the alleged errors result from one cataloger reporting to OCLC that the code interpretation of another cataloger is in error and supplying documentation to verify his/her contention. In this instance, the paraprofessional is not only called upon to assign error, but also to choose between alternative rule interpretations made by professionals. If the paraprofessional is indeed capable of this kind of discriminating judgment simply by consulting detailed guidelines developed by network catalogers, then it is hard to believe that code interpretation is really a professional task. If, on the other hand, code interpretation is complex and requires advanced training in librarianship, then the OCLC assignment of error tallies to library assistants is an unjustified delegation of power. Either interpretation provides evidence of the weakened status of the cataloger in relation to the network and its library assistants. Given this situation, it is quite surprising that this OCLC use of paraprofessionals has evoked virtually no response or protest from catalogers. What does upset many catalogers, however, is that one of their peers has evaluated their work and reported to OCLC that it is substandard. Cataloger reaction to this new level of criticism is discussed in greater detail elsewhere in this book.

BMS both reacts to error reports sent to it and initiates several online proactive activities. Richard Greene, Head of the Section, has named them "search and destroy missions" (Oglebay, 1983:44). They usually refer to global scans of the data base looking for common errors (e.g. such as tagging the United States for listing in the personal name index), or revising outdated spellings in subject headings, or looking for incorrect publication dates (a 1982 scan of the data base for records of printed books with publication dates prior to 1450 had produced more than 6000 citations).

The most emotion-laden activity of BMS is the error tally. In the early 1970's Ohio institutions were the only members of OCLC. They formed a committee to set standards that recommended the formation of a peer council of five catalogers to monitor adherence to standards. After three years' work, the peer council recommended that error reports sent by one library against another library's records be analyzed on a regular basis in order to provide data for calculating an error rate. The error rate was set at the number of member errors, divided by the number of member records input times 100. The peer council also recommended that an unacceptable error rate would be one that was double the system-wide error rate or worse. This formula is still in effect at OCLC but is being considered for revision.

At OCLC the professional librarians in the Bibliographic Maintenance Section take the quarterly records of errors and code them into three categories: "typographical," "other," and "not tallied." "Other" is usually the category where variations from AACR2 or Library of Congress practice occur. "Not tallied" takes in minor errors in coding or in punctuation that do not affect ability to locate the record in the data base. The OCLC staff members forward the error tallies to regional networks. These networks have the right to recalculate the tally using their own categories. Therefore, even within OCLC, calculation of error tallies may vary greatly. However, in general, errors are classified into a scheme similar to the one used by Schoenung (1981: 95–97):

1. Fatal errors—those preventing retrieval of the record because of flaws in the search keys (author, title, Library of Congress card number, etc.).
2. Serious errors—duplicate records or records that contain flaws in parts of the record that are not part of the search keys. Errors in this category contain flaws in describing the material, but those flaws do not prevent searchers from finding some record for the desired item.
3. Minor—every other type of error.

In 1977, OCLC created the Internetwork Quality Control Council (IQCC) to replace the cataloging peer council and act as "... an umbrella peer council for all regional networks" (Oglebay, 1983: 54). The IQCC was requested by the Board of Trustees to analyze error tally mechanisms, to monitor library error rates and to recommend sanctions for nonadherence to network standards. But when IQCC responded by proposing explicit sanctions against offending libraries, the board rejected its work and soon after disbanded the committee. According to many comments by participants at the Oglebay Quality Control Conference held in 1982, this reaction occurred because library administrators opposed direct sanctions against their cataloging departments as an improper extension of network power. While this cannot be confirmed by any of the public documents of the OCLC network, no one denies the fact that the Board of Trustees, having given IQCC a mandate to develop sanctions, backed off from actively imposing them when the User Council (composed primarily of high level library administrators) rejected the IQCC report on sanctions as a counterproductive and unduly combative approach to controlling poor cataloging (OCLC. Users Council, Jan. 25, 1980). Since that time OCLC has adopted the stance that its job is to monitor its data base and encourage its members to police their own production. Schoenung (1981:82) feels that the rejection of IQCC proposed sanctions is only one of many instances where OCLC management's concerned response to administrators has overridden planned programs to enhance data base quality. In his dissertation on the quality of OCLC records, Schoenung analyzed a random sample of items added to the data base between 1971–77. His study produced these amazing results (1981:16):

In all 16,186 errors and variations from LC copy were identified in the 1107 sample records, with the average member-input record containing 14.6 errors. Only nine of the sample records were without any errors and the variation of errors within records was substantial, with "errors" tending to "clump" in certain records. The average record had 0.62 fatal errors, 0.32 serious errors, 10.9 minor errors...
...The most visible deficiency of the OCLC data base is the high incidence of duplicate errors. It is estimated that as many as one in six of the monographic records is in fact a duplicate.

The existence of almost 15 errors in the average record would seem on the face of it to be an indictment of overall cataloging quality and a direct threat to the catalogers' claims that they maintain high standards. In fact, Schoenung's research did not support this view. Further analysis of the records revealed that errors were being assigned to library cataloging on the basis of current standards, whereas the bibliographic records had been created when other LC cataloging and/or OCLC input rules had been in force. In an allied research document also focusing on OCLC record quality, Christian M. Boissonas (1979) divided his sample into Library of Congress and non–Library of Congress records. Even the LC records contained an average of 1.3 inconsistencies with the then prevailing OCLC standard. This pattern of LC errors is supported by internal network research at both RLIN and WLN. At WLN a sample of 97 LC records revealed 41 that conflicted with WLN cataloging standards and interpretations of LC's own rules. At RLIN, it was discovered that at every error sampling taken, LC scored the highest of any institution. This is really not surprising since it is the institution with the largest number of records in the data base. Therefore, this large number of flawed records still represents only a small percentage of LC's total contribution to the data base. These records do indicate, however, that national standard copy is far from perfect.

In all the networks old records, input under previous standards, suddenly become "errors" because of the constantly shifting standards of the Library of Congress and the bibliographic utilities. The pace of change in developing new programs for machine-readable records ensures that "errors" will continue to abound. While the networks need to control and "search and destroy" these faulty records, they are aware that a substantial portion of their problem is traceable not to cataloger error, but to system changes. The changing codes are another major reason why networks avoid sanctions against even the most offending libraries and why quality control personnel have gone on record to warn administrators about the pitfalls of using the error record as the basis of punitive action against catalogers.

This does not mean, however, that OCLC and the regional networks through which it operates have completely backed away from efforts to promote compliance with network standards. What appears to be occurring is a shift from sanctions to praise for, and publicity about, "good" catalogers. In addition, more time has been allocated to the training and retraining of cataloging department personnel. All of the regional networks assist in the training of new libraries in the system and the retraining of catalogers when staff changes occur. Many of the networks also have developed buddy systems whereby libraries with low original input, or with high error rates, place their cataloging in a "Save" file. These records are not transmitted to the network data base. Instead they are accessed and reviewed online either by regional network personnel or by a master cataloger at another library. Errors found in the file are marked for corrections. Only the corrected copy is transmitted to the network catalog. In OCLC Western, this concept of the buddy system is being expanded because it is proving to be a cost-effective quality control check and because it helps to develop ties of loyalty to the network. The buddy system review also provides the network with excellent feedback on common problem areas within the system.

OCLC and the other networks have developed rewards to encourage the compliance of both catalogers and administrators. Commendations for low error rates are bestowed by several of the regional networks affiliated with OCLC and publicity is focused on the work of superior cataloging departments. The Pittsburgh Regional Library Center, for instance, presents annual awards for low error rates. The Fred award (named after OCLC founder Fred Kilgour, and touted by the network as cataloging's equivalent of the movie Oscar), is always presented to the director of the winning library in order to increase his/her appreciation of the efforts of his/her cataloging department to comply with OCLC rules. In describing the impact of this approach, a network representative "... noted that the reaction of the last winner had been amazement, and that his statement of acceptance had included a commitment to more consideration for his technical services department" (Oglebay, 1983:22).

Two of the networks have adopted another approach to quality control which is strongly linked to the cooperative nature of the cataloging networks. At OCLC and WLN, libraries have been identified, through online review of records, as having a high level of quality cataloging. At OCLC, under Project Enhance, 20 of the cataloging departments of these libraries were empowered in February 1984 to correct faulty records of other libraries without going through the intermediary services and second-level checking of OCLC's BMC. These libraries were made responsible for assigning and reporting errors made by other institutions. At WLN, a new category of "Superior" is about to be initiated. Libraries in this rank will be subject to periodic revision of a sample of their records, but, unlike all other WLN members, they will not be subject to revision of every record produced. These changes are notable because in both instances it is the network that assigns the rank and establishes the quality of the individual library cataloging department. In the case of Project Enhance, it should also be noted that the network-selected cataloging departments now wield authority delegated not by the employing institution, but by the network.

While it is clear that networks differ markedly in their approach to quality control of cataloging, it is also evident that they have all developed policies and techniques to encourage and enforce compliance with their institutional norms. The variations in their policies stem naturally from their history, size, and clientele. RLIN, the network with the most prestigious constituency, has less power and less desire to actively monitor records than either of its two competitors. WLN, being the network with the fewest research libraries, has designated for itself the right to check and correct errors. OCLC, treading the middle course, has the greatest mix of libraries and the most varied approach to correcting errors, rewarding compliance and developing guidelines for outsiders (non-OCLC personnel) to use in interpreting network programs, policies, and standards.

Finally, all networks base their quality control activities on the visibility of the online record. It is the visibility feature that allows them to identify both "errors" and "superior" cataloging. Both catalogers and network staffers are aware of the vastly expanded critical audience that network visibility creates. One cataloger graphically described his department's reaction to this new situation in this way: "When each library did its own cataloging for itself, mistakes were seen only by the people within the family, so to speak. Now, if we do a sloppy job, our sins are spread out for everyone to see, magnified by the impartial green and white eyes of the terminal" (Scherba, 1974:31). And Carol Davis of OCLC reminded serials catalogers that (Oglebay, 1983:92)

We do have the capability of looking at an institution's input day-by-day and seeing exactly what you are doing. We can watch you. It's very expensive and time consuming to do it, but we can do it. If we find an institution that seems to be really out in left field with something we may go and look at all their input, get in touch with the (regional) network and the network can take it from there on what needs to be done. I really view this as an educational process: we don't want to be punitive. We've talked though about having terminals that emitted electric shocks when you input a duplicate!

But whether the network action is as direct as an electric shock or as subtle as a Fred award, its underlying purpose is to compel catalogers to adhere to network-required cataloging standards and work rules.

CHAPTER II

Professional and Organizational Control in the Workplace: Review of the Literature

There is an enormous body of literature analyzing the distinguishing traits and claims to status of professional groups. This literature ranges from general surveys of the professions and their power to very detailed analyses of the structure of specific professions, or the reasons why certain occupations have been unable to attain professional status. Since this literature is so vast, it would clearly be impossible to survey all of it in one chapter of this book. What I've attempted instead is to discuss the concepts propounded by some of the most relevant authors and to selectively focus on those characteristics of professionals most likely to be affected by visibility and/or networks.

There is also a relatively large body of literature discussing the professional attributes of librarians. In general, it provides few new insights into the role and functions of professionals. It does, however, reveal concern for creating a rationale to justify the claims to professional rank that librarians have made. On the other hand, the handful of writings about the cataloging subgroup within librarianship reflect less concern over status and more interest in how and why catalogers develop their codes and standards.

Finally, there is an extensive sociological literature examining the relationship of professionals to their employing institutions. The standards developed by these employing organizations to control, monitor, and evaluate the work of professionals and the process whereby these standards change from quality control measures into forces for social control and

sometimes then convert into agents promoting deprofessionalization are all topics covered in this selective literature review.

Research Literature on Professionals

The literature on professionals is dominated by the models
taken from the oldest, most prestigious, and best paying professions—medicine and law. However, as Wilensky (1964) has
shown, other occupations, such as nursing and architecture,
are increasingly laying claim to professional status. Librarianship, for instance, is one such occupation. Ironically, soci-
ologists, the group of academics that have assigned to themselves
the definition of professionalism, also fall into this aspirant
category. Roth (1974:17) thinks that one reason they are so
involved in studying the growth of new professions is "... that
they too are in an occupation on the make and they have an
interest in seeing how they can increase their score in relation
to other occupations."

Wilensky (1964:138) says that there are two distinct and
simple criteria for professionalism:

1. The job of the professional is technical—based on systematic knowledge or doctrine acquired only through long prescribed training.
2. The professional adheres to a set of professional norms.

Research has also shown that professionals are characterized
by the nature of their relationships with colleagues (Greenwood, 1957; Alex, 1969; Mulkay and Williams, 1971). Wilensky
(1964:142) says that colleague control is one of the major characteristics of the accepted professions. He quotes Everett Hughes
who noted that, "The ... quack is the man who continues through
time to please his customers but not his colleagues" (Wilensky,
1964:154; from Hughes, 1958:98). He also isolates two standards which are highly adhered to and accepted in the well-
established professions (1964:138–139):

1. Do what you can to maintain professional standards of work (i.e.
   professionals tend to honor the technical competence of the formally
   qualified, avoid criticism of colleagues in public, condemn un-

qualified practitioners, avoid too much or too little work if it lowers standards).

2. Be aware of the limited competence of your own specialty within the profession, honor the claims of other specialties, and be ready to refer clients to a more competent colleague.

Wilensky stresses that the degree of professionalism of an occupation is defined not only by the claim to exclusive technical competence, but also (1964:139) "... by the degree of adherence to the service ideal and its supporting norms of professional conduct." Because there is public acceptance of the professional's superior knowledge base and commitment to service, this worker is able to attain professional autonomy, the right to determine the nature of problems to be addressed, the techniques and methods for solving them, and the evaluation of that problem solving by other professionals.

Finally, Wilensky places great emphasis on the middle range of learning that the professional knowledge base occupies. It is not too precise or too vague, too narrow or too broad. Professionals concern themselves with ambiguous, complex, and sometimes conflicting concepts. Their specialized training and education uniquely equips them to make decisions within gray areas of human understanding and activity.

Almost every writer on the professions cites Wilensky's two criteria for professionalism, his emphasis on collegial relationships, and his overview of the factors required for an occupation to evolve into a profession. Other noted studies examine in great detail specific attributes of professionalism. Among the most discussed are:

1. The ability to define who is in and who is out of the profession (Hall, 1968; Freidson, 1970; Jamous and Peloille, 1970; Perrucci and Gerstl, 1969). In a Pulitzer Prize–winning study, Paul Starr (1983) describes how physicians achieved ascendancy in American health care industries and how their status is now being threatened by profit-making corporations run by managers who have little or no medical training. In general, these studies show that professions protect their autonomy by creating a set of ethical codes, establishing educational requirements for entry, and developing licen-

sing procedures that specify what it takes to enter the professional group (Borricaud, 1979).

2. The emergence of one dominant professional association, recognized as competent to speak authoritatively for the profession. Gilb (1966) demonstrates how associations now exercise considerable political control and often successfully lobby for professional interests, even when they run contrary to the public interest. Many writers feel that without the professional association, there would be no way to develop the collective power required to insure that the profession's boundary-setting efforts would be successful.

3. The dominance of individual achievement, protected and supported by collective effort (Larson, 1977:xvii, 156–243) calls professions a form of structured inequality because they rely on built-in inequities of access to education and built-in differences in economic and intellectual ability to provide the primary sources for screening out applicants.

4. The requirement of educational standards that exceed the real knowledge required to perform most professional tasks (Reader, 1966; Friedman, 1965). Pauline Wilson's rationale for this practice is that in this way the profession is able to "protect the intelligence of the whole." Every member of the profession acquires an overview of its history, its ethics, and its various specialities: "With the division of labor which makes mechanization possible, skilled workers lost their capacity to comprehend the entire process of production. When they lost that capacity, they lost control of their work. By protecting the intelligence of the whole, professions are able to maintain control of their work" (1981:287).

5. Control of the market for the profession's services. The profession, in effect, monopolizes its market and sets not only the standards for entry, but also the procedures and techniques for delivering service. The attribute of control of the market is not true of all professions and is generally less likely to occur in occupations striving to become professions. This is one of the reasons why Wilensky is dubious that there will be a great increase in the number of accepted professions. He asserts that many of these occupations are dependent upon bureaucracies which " ... enfeeble the service ideal" (1964:147) and often demand a market orientation (as opposed to a service orientation) from their employees. Thus the impact of bureaucracies on professionals and occupations aspiring to be professional is considered by many writers to be extremely negative (Blakenship, 1980; Hall, 1968).

Librarians as Professionals

Whether or not librarians can lay claim to joining the ranks of professionals has been a topic of intense interest to these information workers for many years. The mere fact that librarians often insist on the word "professional" in their titles is one indication of their lack of confidence in this claim. Doctors and lawyers, working at the pinnacle of the professions, almost never bother to add that word to their titles because the occupational titles subsume the professional category.

Indeed, a fairly strong argument can be made that librarians are not true professionals. Professional authority and status rest in part on the mystique associated with technical expertise and the ability to provide a satisfying rationale for imposing occupational standards of practice. Several studies have shown that librarians do not have control over an esoteric body of knowledge (Goode, 1961; North, 1977). In general, the training provided by library schools lacks the abstractness and rigor usually associated with legal or medical education. Far more important, librarians lack monopoly over a knowledge base since many nonprofessionals (e.g. academics, researchers, and computer specialists) have highly developed skills and training for organizing, locating, and distributing information (Shaffer, 1968).

Prolonged and specialized training is not even an absolute requirement for work as a librarian. As a rule, librarians are not licensed and sometimes they are not even required to be graduates of accredited training programs (Ryan, 1967). In the 1983 Merwine versus Mississippi State University court case, a jury ruled that Mississippi State could not establish the requirement that applicants for librarians' positions possess library degrees from American Library Association–accredited schools. This ruling has been appealed, but should it be upheld, it will undoubtedly undermine the status of librarians, graduate library schools, and the American Library Association (Edward G. Holley, 1984). At present, neither librarians nor their recognized professional association, the American Library Association, possess the legal authority to enforce minimum standards of entry into the occupation or conformity to a code of ethics. Indeed, the whole structure of the American Library Association defies the traditional concept of a professional organization, for it requires no credentials for admittance, tends to blur jurisdictional lines that might separate librarians from nonlibrarians, and has never been able to define a theoretical arena reserved solely for librarians. Because of these conditions, control over employment—hiring, promotion, and evaluation—rests primarily with employers and far less with colleagues or the professional association. One analyst has noted that: "Without an effective monopoly over educational services, without the [legal] recognition and support of the state, and without a capacity to take collective action, the occupation is unable to enforce compliance with occupational standards of practice." (Reeves, 1981:141).

Despite these overwhelmingly negative factors, this same analyst concludes, after studying 36 libraries and library systems, that librarians probably are professional because they have been able to develop a collective occupational orientation (1981:143):

The causal and moral texture of the institutions of librarianship gives a sense of purpose and consequence to activities.

Those familiar with the standards and principles of librarianship acknowledge a distinct hierarchy of occupational authority and responsibility centering on the professional librarian. Those who recognize the relevance of these standards and principles, and yet are unfamiliar with their specifics, defer to the judgment of librarians.

Whether professional status can be confirmed by evidence proving that librarians are listened to, or have authority in some organizational settings, is questionable. Some practitioners have sidestepped making judgments on this issue by placing librarianship in the realm of a semi-profession. (Wilensky [1964] places it among professions in process of attempting to attain full status; Denzin [1968] links it to optometry, osteopathy, and chiropracty as examples of incomplete professionalism; Goode [1961] says that its weak knowledge base makes librarianship only marginally professional). They argue that it is best to think of professionalism as a continuum ranging from those occupations that have all the characteristics associated with professionalism (autonomy, self-policing ethics, monopoly of market, utilization of a common body of knowledge requiring extended training to acquire, goals of community service) to those where one or more of these elements may be missing, usually either autonomy or monopoly of market (Murray S. Martin, 1981:75–93).

Whether or not librarians are semi-, demi-, or wholly professionals, there is no arguing with the fact that they are greatly concerned with the concept of professionalism not only because they seek improved status, but also because of their strong commitment to a service ideal. Meyer argues that the librarian's power within organizations is weak and professional status could never be claimed on the basis of autonomy. The only way to become professional is "... to internalize and accentuate the service attitude, to assume a professional demeanor, and to pursue self-esteem and status on the basis of good service rather than artificial attachments" (1980:281). By "artificial attachments," Meyer means general attributes of professionalism that appear to be lacking in librarianship. For this reason, he attacks AACR2 as a sham created to provide outsiders with proof that librarians do possess the requisite esoteric knowledge required of professionals (1980:281):

It is possible that the new cataloging code (620 pages) was created because it takes as many rules as writ therein to catalog library materials. It is equally possible that a more subtle need, that we own a body of knowledge unique to the profession, is the real reason we have this complex set of rules which only a few can fully understand.

Veaner (1985:223) provides a new way to define library professionalism—to state what professionals should not do and then make sure that librarians avoid these activities. Veaner particularly wants to remove "production/manufacturing work" which he equates with practically all library technical services and most particularly with specialized original cataloging.

Once this occurs librarians can concentrate on their true professional roles as (1985:228) "intermediaries, teachers, consultants, advisors, and interpreters" of the store of information in the library collection. Carrying Veaner's idea to its logical extreme, it would appear that librarians can only retain their claim to professionalism by eliminating about half of the activities now designated as professional work.

Birdsall also stresses developing new definitions for library professionalism. He argues (1982:225) that there is a new kind of professional emerging, one who will focus on making clients self sufficient, and the librarian is becoming this kind of professional. Pauline Wilson (1981) offers another solution to the failure to develop many professional characteristics, especially work autonomy, and that is to strengthen the professional association. As its power grows, it will be able to provide autonomy for its members.

Thus many library writers offer justifications and rationales for the absence of critical professional attributes (e.g. autonomy, esoteric knowledge base, strong professional association). Whatever the merit of their arguments may be, it is clear that lacking these characteristics severely undermines the power and status of this group of workers.

Catalogers as Professionals

Librarians, like marginal professionals in general, can be characterized as having great concern about status. Catalogers, of course, share this concern and appear to stake all their claims to being professionals on their ability to define and refine work standards and rules, thereby creating the esoteric knowledge that Meyer cynically commented on. But, unlike Meyer, catalogers genuinely believe in their codes and the intellectual training that helped develop them. Therefore, many catalogers and other librarians view this librarian subgroup as a breed apart, characterized by a need for more autonomy and more emphasis on collegial evaluation. Whether this perception is a realistic one for catalogers working in a network environment is one of the topics of my research.

Although very little analysis has been devoted to the process by which catalogers define their occupation, many contributors to library literature assume as a given that catalogers are concerned with a Platonic vision of a perfect record and an almost obsessive regard for how they are ranked by their peers. In particular, other librarians, especially those dealing directly with the public in reference or administrative functions, often comment bitterly that their cataloging colleagues have substituted means for ends. Thus Toohey and Biermann (1964:3698–3699) note:

> The art of cataloging is a great deal like the art of gargoyle carving. It is a satisfying and ennobling labor, allowing the cataloger full exertion of his mental faculties and free play of his imagination. The end result is full of divergencies and, to the eye of everyone but the cataloger himself, often grotesque.... Just as the worshippers of Saint Pierre have no real concern about the aesthetics of gargoyles as long as they look like gargoyles and effectively drain the roof, the users of libraries are for the most part oblivious of our most cherished cataloging niceties.

In 1961, Draper (1964:1907) decided to organize research to test the generally held belief "... that catalogers catalog for other catalogers, just as many believe that women dress to impress other women rather than the putative audience." Draper selected a cataloging practice, the use of brackets around the publication date on the catalog card to signify that the date does not appear on the title page, and then surveyed a group of 70 graduate students to determine if anyone knew what the brackets stood for. None of the graduate students correctly identified the reason for this practice or the meaning of the brackets. Draper then went on to survey heads of academic library cataloging departments, informing them of the results of his research and asking for their response to an alternative rule that would clarify the source of the publication date. Of the 35 responses received, more than two-thirds ignored the existence of the library user and emphasized that catalogers found brackets useful devices for description of non–title page information. Most replies also stressed the importance of following agreed-upon rules, regardless of their utility to the patron. One cataloger commented that "American cataloging rules have always used the title page as the basis for descriptive cataloging. The 'purpose' or 'usefulness' of this practice is not known, nor is it pertinent" (1964:1910). Draper contended that

his research had uncovered a new disease, "bibliothecal so-
lipsism" (1964:1910):

It is the implicit belief that libraries exist for the sake of the activity
known as librarianship, and that shadowy figures from the Outside
who wander about the catalog with a bewildered look are Aliens whose
main function is to get in the way of librarians.
To be sure, most librarians are free of the disease. Also most miners
do not get silicosis. But, especially in view of the widespread belief
that catalogers tend to be most susceptible to its ravages, it may be
useful to point with alarm.

Not everyone views the catalogers' indifference to patron
values with this same level of distress. In "Question of Motive"
(1976), Pince compares catalogers and detectives and concludes
that they both share the traits of searching for truth, regardless
of the consequences to others, and are also characterized by an
inherent and sustaining belief in their own righteousness. This
faith enables them to perform at high efficiency when given a
high level of autonomy.

On the other hand, catalogers experience great frustration
in work settings where that autonomy is restricted or denied.
A 1976 survey of 350 librarians in 94 university libraries (Chwe,
1976) revealed substantial differences between reference librarians and catalogers on two subdimensions of overall job
satisfaction. Reference librarians were less satisfied than catalogers with their pay, and catalogers were more dissatisfied
than reference librarians about the moral values of their job—
they felt forced to do things at work that contravened their
professional standards and codes.

It appears then that this subgroup of library professionals is
characterized by fascination with its own rules and knowledge
base and by its belief in the necessity for collegial evaluation.

Professionals in Bureaucratic Organizations

Although professionalism is not necessarily incompatible with
work in bureaucratic organizations, most writers and researchers do stress that the work arrangements in these institutions

usually weaken professional autonomy. Large organizations, modeled along bureaucratic lines, have been described by Max Weber (1964, edited by Talcott Parsons) and his many followers as a hierarchical chain of command, with clearly defined duties at each level and goals and procedures determined by top administrators. This type of institution naturally develops a system that discourages autonomy and innovation in the ranks. The professional in such a setting becomes a functionary of the bureaucracy.

Of course bureaucracies vary in their organization and delegation of authority to occupational groups. One of the most interesting modern organizational developments is the growth of the professional organization. Bucher and Stelling (1980) state that the professional organization should not be confused with the professional association. The latter institution sets standards and monitors entry into, and behavior within, the entire profession. The professional organization, on the other hand, consists of one institution, often employing many types of professionals (e.g. a hospital may use the services of doctors, lawyers, and social workers), and also many paraprofessionals and clerks. Bucher and Stelling (1980) assert that in this type of specialized bureaucratic organization, professionals exert considerable influence and control. Hospitals, social work agencies, and libraries are among the institutions that appear to fall into this category.

Academic institutions are often cited as examples of professional organizations (Caplow and McGee, 1958; Mulkay and Williams, 1971). Over the years they have acquired the elaborate machinery required to mediate between competing groups and to integrate the professional requirements of the various interests they encompass. This integration is achieved through a continuous political process. University statutes and constitutions define in general terms the role and obligations of the faculty and administration and then provide the mechanisms (committees, forums, senates, etc.) to resolve competing viewpoints and interests.

In a 10–year study of six major medical institutions, Bucher and Stelling (1980:132) concluded that "... there is a strong tendency for non-academic professional organizations to develop some of these legislative forms." In particular they stressed the development of peer groups, acting through committees to establish professional standards and norms within the organization. They also noted, however, that "... different occupational groupings achieve more or less professional status, and with their measure of success, they achieve more or less influence in an organization" (1980:138). Social workers, a relatively weak professional group, were characterized as having practically no control over the overall goals of the employing institution and much less autonomy than physicians in specifying how their work was to be accomplished or evaluated. This point of view was confirmed by Hall's (1968) study of professionals working for large organizations. It showed that the degree of control of professionals by organizations is highly variable and will change over time as new factors (i.e. the introduction of technology) are introduced into the work environment.

Regardless of whether work is being done in a traditionally bureaucratic or a professional setting, organizations affect professionals as well as being affected by them. They provide the framework for their careers and influence their professional identities and values (Freidson, 1970; Hall, 1968). They are the intermediaries between the professional and the marketplace. In so doing, they often place pressure on professionals to become more responsive to the demands of the public for less costly access to professional services (Blishen, 1969), and/or for some measure of accountability by professionals to consumers rather than their professional associations and colleagues.

Organizations as Agents for Social Control of Professionals

Economists have traditionally treated the "invisible hand" of the marketplace as an important societal control device which helps reward efficiency and stimulate innovation. Although most economic analysts have focused on profit-making industries, organizations that provide public services, such as hospitals and libraries, also must respond to their markets if they wish to remain viable. In this context, social control within organizations means that standards of performance and expectations of behavior are part of a collective public process involving consumers as well as administrators and also including the providers of goods and services.

Zald (1976) says that social control includes four elements:

1. The formulation and dissemination of standards of performance.
2. The surveillance of performance.
3. The sanctioning or reinforcement of desirable behavior, sometimes involving identification of moral examplars.
4. The discovery and punishment of deviance, which is defined as the failure to meet norms.

According to Zald (1976:15–17), visibility is one of the key elements affecting the organization's power to enforce its standards. The ability to monitor performance is dependent upon the visibility of the behavior, product, or service that is associated with the organizational standard. If deviance can be identified, then sanctions can be applied. Professional associations usually control symbolic sanctions (e.g. withdrawal of a license), whereas professional organizations and other bureaucracies can apply punishments as direct as firing an employee. Despite this, Glaser (1964) and other researchers have demonstrated that organizations that place primary emphasis on professional self-monitoring rather than sanctions develop the highest degree of organizational loyalty and productivity from their professional workers.

Zald also discusses two other reasons why sanctions may prove one of the less effective control mechanisms for professional workers:

1. Surveillance and/or making visible a service may be expensive, or the cost of enforcing sanctions may be high. In these instances, the organization may choose to ignore known violations.
2. Surveillance and/or sanctions might destroy the original purpose of a program (e.g. refusing to reaccredit a hospital might permanently damage the total quality of neighborhood health services).

Within organizations, be they bureaucratic or professional, employees affected by work standards may resist compliance.

They may lobby, evade, and organize in perceived self-defense against unacceptable standards (Reisman and Rohrer, 1957; Scott, 1964). Such action is particularly true of professionals who have been trained to rely on their own judgments or on collegial and peer group review to provide quality control of their work (Perrucci and Gerstl, 1969).

Finally, organizational behavior is often changed by the difference between the intended effect of an action (e.g. making work visible) and its unanticipated results (e.g. creating blacklists of poor workers). Zald and Hair (1972), for instance, show that the attempt of established surgeons to limit entry into their field ultimately resulted in public regulation of hospital performance and the development of accreditation standards.

At any rate, standards, sanctions, and deviance in organizations are only operative in relation to some visible work activity, or some artifact of a service being provided. Researchers find that when such visible activity occurs, or when work previously invisible is made visible, fascinating results develop. Stelling and Bucher (1972) describe how establishing tissue committees in hospitals, designed to monitor the organs and tissue removed during operations, has resulted in declines in the number of amputations that doctors perform. They also provide evidence that psychiatrists and other doctors have created a vast repertoire of techniques to hide or prevent discovery of professional mistakes and failures. Rose Coser (1961) looks at changes in managerial practices when professionals lose insulation from observability and concludes that, in general, managers seek to avoid directly confronting professionals with evidence of their mistakes. Donald Ball (1974) analyzes the relationship of visibility to replacement rates and rewards of professional football players and concludes that the more visible the player's position, the more likely he is to be replaced. On the other hand, he is compensated for this increased vulnerability by having a higher salary than players in less exposed positions.

Thus in any context, visibility is an important component of organizational control and accountability. One aspect of this social control within organizations is that it rests with the authority able or willing to impose punishments for deviance and provide rewards for compliance.

Deprofessionalization

The growing use of technology, especially the dependence on computers, is a dominant theme of any study of modern American organizations. Peter Drucker (1969), for instance, has asserted that a new kind of society is emerging, the postindustrial or knowledge society. In this society, the collection, organization, and application of information becomes more important than the production of goods. If this view is correct, information professionals, like librarians, should experience increased status and security. This is also the viewpoint stressed in Daniel Bell's (1973) influential book *The Coming of Post Industrial Society*. In that book Bell contends that the emerging new society will be characterized by its emphasis on theoretical knowledge and this will sharply contrast with the primary stress on empirical knowledge that characterizes industrial society. The growing capabilities of computers will lead to an intellectual technology and its reflection in such activities as systems analysis, decision making, and other problem-solving techniques. Because of the emphasis on knowledge, professionals (groups acknowledged to possess monopolies on specific subject areas) will become more dominant in society and will therefore be better able to control their own spheres of activity.

This rosy prospect for professionals is not the unanimous view of futurists. In fact, many analysts are extremely critical of this vision. They agree that technology, automation, and computers will dominate organizational and professional work activities. They argue, however, that this combination of forces will create a vastly different result—the deprofessionalization of the information society.

Nina Toren (1975) contends that technological changes often result in making professional knowledge less esoteric and special. In some cases, it becomes available simply by pushing a button. When this happens, society refuses to recognize the professional's claim to special treatment on the grounds that he/she possesses a unique knowledge base. Montagna (1968) provides a specific illustration of this process in his study of certified public accountants. Much of a CPA's work can now be taken over by computers, thus significantly curtailing the scope of professional judgment and the risk involved in making decisions. As Montagna notes, occupations whose decisions entail little risk or uncertainty will have a hard time maintaining professional status.

Computers also threaten professional status in other ways. Professionals come to rely upon computers for the generation of the data that they use. As a result, they become more dependent upon computer technicians and specialists for access to information in their fields. But those computer technicians are now capable of making the information known not only to the professional practitioner, but also directly to the client. Thus Gershuny (1977) finds evidence in the present service society of a relentless trend to a future self-service society. And Marie Haug (1975:205) stresses in her article, "The Deprofessionalization of Everyone?", that knowledge no longer needs to be "... packed only in the professional's head or in a specialized library where it is relatively inaccessible. It can be available not only to those who know, but to those who know how to get it."

Lopata (1976) contends that the proliferation of experts and the increased specialization required by a complex technology reduces the distinctive role of the professional and blurs the distinction between the professional and the technician. It then becomes increasingly difficult for the public to understand or support the enhanced status of the professional in relation to the paraprofessional or technician. Yarmolinsky (1978) found evidence of this process in his analysis of trends affecting professionals. Thus studies of deprofessionalization show that the professional suffers because:

1. Work previously reserved for professionals is made routine and subdivided among workers with less formal education and training. Denzin (1968) notes that many medicines are now ready-made and

simply need to be pulled from a shelf. Such developments lessen belief in the need to employ pharmacists to provide most drugs.

2. More demands for accountability (meeting production and quality standards) by clients and/or employers emerge. These consumers of professional services have developed more access to knowledge and are therefore more confident of their ability to judge professional work. Zola and Miller (1973) describe this process and its effects on doctors' prestige, status, and autonomy.

If these studies are correct, technology may provide the foundation for both the information society and the deprofessionalization of the information profession. If so, one would naturally expect that the status of librarians would be negatively affected. Indeed, the following review of library literature does reveal evidence of possible trends toward deprofessionalization of librarianship in general, and of cataloging in particular.

Deprofessionalization of Cataloging

In recent years, library literature has been filled with articles finding evidence of the withering away of cataloging as a professional activity. Holley (1981) forecasts that future emphasis in cataloging will be placed on the sharing of high-quality bibliographic records available through networks. Original cataloging in almost every library will decrease. The work of the professional will not primarily be to catalog, but to supervise departments composed of paraprofessionals who do almost all the cataloging for the library. Kochen and Segur (1970) develop a mathematical model to justify having the Library of Congress do as much as possible of all the original cataloging in the United States. They assert that the increased cost of computers and network services will be more than offset by the potential nationwide savings resulting from the decreased need for catalogers. Kennedy (1980) reviews recent and anticipated advances in library automation and technology, focusing especially on the impact of OCLC, MARC formatting, and AACR2. Her analysis leads her to predict an increase in the technical qualifications required for those few catalogers who would be doing original cataloging and participating in the development of standards, combined with a large decrease in the overall number of catalogers. Kayner (1978) compared the cost of copy cataloging (accepting or editing cataloging records in the data base) done primarily by paraprofessionals to the original cataloging done primarily by professionals. Her conclusion was that costs might be reduced by as much as 30 percent if administrators placed more emphasis on using copy cataloging and deterred their catalogers from making intensive efforts to change the network records. Braden, Hall, and Britten (1980) analyzed a survey of 147 OCLC-member libraries. Results disclosed a trend toward less professional revision of network-available copy and increased use of paraprofessionals and clerks to produce cataloging records. The National Library of Canada (1974) study of the economics of shared cataloging was based on an extensive time-motion analysis and revealed that it is far cheaper to edit an existing network record at $0.12 a record than to key in original cataloging at $1.43 per record.

Koel (1981) reviewed catalog use studies and concluded that they all revealed that a catalog designed to act solely as a finding tool would satisfy 75–90 percent of academic library users. He argued therefore that bibliographic records are probably too detailed and that the time spent and standards developed by catalogers to create authority controls and consistency in the catalog were probably not justifiable and might well be eliminated. Druschel (1981) described a comparative cost analysis at the Washington State University Libraries using a bibliographic utility (WLN) as compared to a manual system of cataloging. Eleven more staff members and 1365 more staff hours were required per month to process the same amount of materials in the manual system as were processed through the automated system. Perhaps even more important, the automated records were found to be more accurate and easier to update than those in the manual system. Such results reinforced Washington State University Library's commitment to increased use of network files. In "The Catalogerless Society" (1983) the claim is made that the present benefits of network cataloging are just the tip of the iceberg. Future sophistication of computer programming will eliminate the need for almost all in-house professional cataloging. Paraprofessionals will be able to insert information copied from the book in hand into the computer which will either locate a record already in the network files or create a record by automatically checking online subject headings files, name authority files, and online cataloging standards. The result will be an acceptable record and a standardized and consistent catalog.

Gorman (1979) provides another perspective and another challenge to the claims of catalogers for unique possession of a specialized body of knowledge. He argues that terminals will soon be accessible throughout libraries and therefore the rationale for segregating cataloging into one department—access to rules, authority lists, collection inventories, etc.—will cease to exist. Once this situation occurs, it should be possible to distribute the small amount of material not located in the network data base to all librarian professionals, and allocate more routine tasks to paraprofessional groups. Gorman's assertion that all library professionals can catalog preserves cataloging as a task of library professionals but does not limit this activity to the cataloging subgroup within the profession. Therefore, it does vastly increase the number of participants in the cataloging process. Moreover, it flies in the face of the professional dictum delineated by Wilensky (1964:141), "Be aware of the limited competence of your own specialty within the profession, honor the claims of other specialties, and be ready to refer clients to a more competent colleague." The implication that all librarians are equally competent in all specialized activities of librarianship may indicate that library training is too generalized and so is unable to develop the middle range professional knowledge base that Wilensky describes.

Undoubtedly, however, the main impetus for reducing the scope, status, and size of cataloging departments comes not from other professionals, but from library administrators. The need to control finances and to provide new services (many of them computer and/or network based) forces administrators to consider ways to reallocate resources. Cataloging is an expensive, labor-intensive activity which many administrators feel can no longer be justified. Richard De Gennaro (1981:1047),

Director of Libraries at the University of Pennsylvania, surveyed the current state of nationwide library budgets and concluded that:

> Traditional cataloging may go the way of hand bookbinding. Hand
> binding was an art and a craft. The work was beautiful and durable,
> but the labor costs involved became prohibitive and we had to learn
> to accept less elegant, but more affordable machine alternatives. With
> production at a few books a day per cataloger, traditional original
> cataloging, like hand binding, has also priced itself out of the market.

Since most libraries prepare very detailed statistics about
every aspect of their activity, it is really surprising how little
data is available about the average production of catalogers.
Many articles, like De Gennaro's, simply assert that it is only
"a few books a day" without providing any evidence. One study,
however, is quite explicit. A comprehensive Canadian study by
Sharon Chapple of the National Library of Canada (1974) cal-
culated that catalogers produce approximately 4.5 cataloging
records daily. This figure includes work required to catalog,
code, and input material into a computerized data base in MARC
format. Overton and Seal (1979) analyzed British University
Library cataloging production statistics. They did not concentrate on average production figures of catalogers, but were interested in the average cost of cataloging a book. Their study
showed that it cost more than half the price of the book to get
it cataloged. Therefore (1979:19) "... if a typical library's cataloging costs could be halved, 25% more books could be bought."
     A somewhat indirect verification of this high cost/low level
production is that most published responses by catalogers to
attacks on the low quantity of their work do not deny low
production, but justify it as a consequence of the growing complexity of catalogers' work and the traditional responsibility of
this group for maintaining the quality of bibliographic records.
Soules (1983:28), for instance, argues forcefully that new codes,
constant revisions, growing inconsistency of Library of Congress cataloging, and the complexity of online cataloging in a
network environment are placing huge new burdens upon the
cataloger:

The use of the computer has not simplified matters, it has complicated them. Nearly every procedure that has been transposed from manual operation to a computer has been complicated—some beyond belief. No one can just sit down and catalog a book anymore. We must think of all these problems as we catalog. Then the book must be coded and input (not just typed). The end product is achieved, but only with increased effort.

At any rate, the high costs of bibliographic control are a continuing source of concern and a goad to innovation by administrators. In his article Ake I. Koel (1981), the Associate Librarian for Technical Services at Yale, posed a question as his title—"Bibliographic Control at the Crossroads: Do We Get Our Money's Worth?"—and answered "probably not." In particular, the utility of the major quality control devices of cataloging, authority files, did not justify their costs. Spyers-Duran (1978) also stressed cost considerations. In 1977 he surveyed 130 head catalogers at large academic libraries. His study revealed that network participation by these libraries had consistently resulted in the reorganization of cataloging departments. This was accompanied by an increasing percentage of cataloging being done by nonprofessionals (80–95 percent). The rise in status of support staff (paraprofessionals vis-à-vis professionals) was especially noteworthy. While sympathetic to the personal trauma this caused many catalogers, Library Director Spyers-Duran hastened to remind them that the productivity of the library took precedence over individual concerns about status (1978:32):

The clerical and paraprofessional staff experienced fuller participation in departmental procedural decisions. Some libraries reported that some of their professional catalogers viewed this development without much enthusiasm. In these cases, the paraprofessionals were assigned the copy cataloging, leaving only the original cataloging for the professionals. It is not difficult to imagine the chagrin of a professional proof-slip cataloger of many years when an assertive nonprofessional assumes previously professional responsibilities on the terminal. While the importance of recognizing and understanding interpersonal issues cannot be overstated, it is equally important to realize that a truly cooperative effort is required to attain any desired goal, and this may require putting personal feelings in their proper perspective and persevering in the most productive direction for the whole organization.

There is a large body of evidence that administrators are becoming more assertive about analyzing cataloging costs and reducing them wherever possible. This trend toward monetary accountability is linked to another movement recently reflected in the library literature—the demand that cataloging services and standards be justified by demonstrated utility to the library patron. In this instance, the catalyzing agent inspiring administrators to revolt against cataloger-inspired standards is the code itself, AACR2. Many library administrators and even some catalogers and some network personnel have questioned the wisdom of adopting this code. Georgia Brown (1981) reported the results of a survey by OCLC which identified 454 changes or new rules resulting from the code revision. Of these, 56 percent would benefit no one, 23 percent would benefit librarians, and only 21 percent would benefit patrons. Martell (1981:7) reported that:

Most likely library administrators failed to support AACR2 because: 1) they were entirely uncertain about its implication costs, 2) they could not justify its benefits to their constituencies, and 3) neither they nor their staff were committed to a code change—it was quite simply an external and bothersome intrusion.

De Gennaro (1981:1047), one of the most influential library directors and contributors to library literature, asserted that:

Shared cataloging on the networks, after an initial burst of productivity, is slowing down as data bases grow and as standards are raised to perfection levels by conscientious catalogers in response to real or imagined network requirements. Meanwhile, the coming of AACR2 is slowing down today's work and forcing us to re-do some of yesterday's. Far from becoming extinct, original cataloging and the catalog maintenance functions in large libraries are now growth industries and AACR2 promises to become cataloging's Full Employment Act.

In reality, De Gennaro's fears have proved groundless. There is no evidence of an increase in cataloging employment resulting from implementation of AACR2. On the other hand, work backlogs, increased use of networks to convert files, and other extra costs are directly traceable to this cataloger-developed code.

Another element in the administrators' revolt stems from the results of numerous surveys of users' responses to a new technological development in libraries, the creation of online catalogs. These catalogs are being implemented to replace the prevalent library index to collections, the card catalog. They will provide users with new ways to search for materials in the libraries' collections, including enhanced ability to search words in titles and to combine subject headings. In general, studies show that patrons react favorably to this new type of catalog, that they are content with a small amount of information on the record (author, title, call number, etc.), and that they intend to use the catalog as a finding, not a bibliographic, tool (Koel, 1981; Tolle et al., 1983; Kaske et al., 1983). Seal's (1983) experimental study, exposing users to very detailed or very short cataloging records for the same item, showed about equal patron satisfaction with both types of record.

Beckman (1982) reported on parallel surveys of users and catalogers, inquiring from both groups their perceptions of what library patrons require and want in an online catalog. The catalogers placed high priority on standards, rational structure, and authority files, whereas users stressed search simplicity and fast response time. Moreover, catalogers ranked cost only as 25th out of 40 priorities in selecting an online catalog system. Even users had ranked it much higher. Presumably if administrators had been surveyed, they would have put it near the top of their lists. Beckman stresses that knowledge of technological developments and careful consideration of all costs were far more essential to administrators planning online catalogs than adherence to cataloging standards or the establishment of online planning priorities by catalogers.

Patrick Wilson (1983) questions the very reason and rationale for the present catalog's existence. He points out that the catalog only helps patrons locate books on shelves. It does not provide a useful guide to the contents of the material in the library nor any measure of the quality of the material located.

Yet this is precisely the kind of task that should (but never has and probably never will) comprise the intellectual enterprise of the professional cataloger. He states that (1983:173): "Librarians and others professionally concerned with information storage and retrieval shy away from the question of quality." Although he is examining library services from an entirely different perspective, he too is concerned with the value of catalogs to patrons and reaches the same general conclusion—in an era of great technological advances, present cataloging standards and goals are out of touch with patrons' perceived and real needs. Such a conclusion challenges the social service concept on which the professional status of the cataloger is based.

Library literature in the 1970's and early 1980's clearly reflects a growing disillusionment with the quality of bibliographic records produced by catalogers, combined with skepticism about the utility of the codes these records were based upon. That same literature also records catalogers responding to these attacks by defending their codes, by explaining away alleged errors in their cataloging, and by developing peer groups to protect catalogers' standards and interests. Kelm (1978) explains the historical factors that led to the development of AACR2 and places emphasis on the legitimate desire of catalogers to establish an internationally accepted standard for bibliographic description. Gorman (1978:209) argues that AACR2 kept cataloging "... if not up-to-date, at least contemporary." McPherson et al. (1982) describe the development of the University of California's online catalog, Melvyl. This catalog is highly popular with users. McPherson is certain that it could not have been created without adherence to highly complex and detailed cataloging standards. Asher feels that the cost of abiding by the new cataloging standard is exaggerated. He asserts (1980:228), "AACR2 and the card catalog can live together—and cheaply." Boissonas (1979) studied a sample of records in the OCLC data base and found that approximately three changes or revisions in each member input record were necessary to create a perfect record. Even Library of Congress records contained an average of 1.3 errors per record. Boissonas uses these data to justify his contention that more, not less, adherence to cataloging codes and standards is required. After all, these codes guarantee consistency in network data bases and provide long term benefits and savings both to libraries and to networks. Library literature is filled with articles describing new uses for computerized bibliographic files. Many of these articles note the important input of interlibrary cooperative cataloging committees and peer groups (Nasatir, 1983; Avram, 1983). Network annual reports and newsletters also note the important role played by cataloging advisory committees. At the Oglebay Quality Control Conference (1982), Richard Greene, Head of OCLC Bibliographic Maintenance Section, reviewed the number of national cataloging advisory committees that OCLC and the other networks rely upon. The other participants at the conference constantly stressed the fact that it was cataloger-developed codes such as MARC that made it possible to create networks. They also believed that cataloger-developed standards would provide the foundation for facilitating the exchange of international bibliographic records.

Thus the literature dealing with the effect of network development on the status of catalogers provides evidence of deprofessionalization (shifting of tasks to nonprofessionals, routinization of tasks, public and administrative skepticism about the group's superior knowledge and public service ideal) alongside a hefty body of reports attesting to the strength of cataloging advisory groups and their success in winning acceptance of even their much maligned codes, such as AACR2. Given these mixed signals from the literature, this case study of how catalogers, administrators, and network personnel perceive the status, the career prospects, and the mission of catalogers in their newly computerized environment was designed to provide a limited, but reality-based, overview of the impact of new technology on catalogers and other endangered specialist groups.

CHAPTER **III**

Deprofessionalization

In five of the six libraries where I interviewed catalogers, administrators, and other staff members there had been an overall decline in the size of the cataloging departments during the past decade. In general, fewer professional catalogers were employed, but the reduction in their numbers was not as great as in the number of clerks whose very routine jobs (e.g. typing catalog cards) had largely been eliminated by the computer. Many deprofessionalizing trends were evident, however. Even in those departments that suffered little or no attrition in the number of professional positions, it was clear that the role and career expectations of the cataloger had greatly diminished. At Stanford, for instance, no new cataloger had been hired for seven years. At San Jose, the last original cataloger had been hired in 1980 and overall the department had suffered a one-third cut in personnel during the past decade. At San Francisco State, the last cataloger had been hired more than 10 years ago; at Sonoma State, over 15 years ago. At Berkeley and the University of Washington, which both have huge libraries, there had been some recent hirings, but for very specialized areas. The overall number of catalogers had declined.

More important than the numbers count was the almost unanimous view expressed by the catalogers that their status in their specific institutions, and in the library profession in general, was in a process of drastic decline. This overwhelming pessimism resulted from a number of factors.

The most striking change in the catalogers' activities emerged directly from the introduction of the computer. In every instance, this action ultimately required physical reorganization of the department so that work flow could center around the machine. But the dominance of the computer was more than a matter of moving furniture. It meant that time schedules and work assignments were geared to the hours established by the networks instead of being determined by the department head or by the catalogers. It also meant that carefully planned production schedules could be, and were, wiped out by computer downtime and network-scheduled maintenance time. If, as in the case of RLIN in 1982, the network system suffered serious deterioration and departments were allotted short daily schedules for network production, all other activities had to be rescheduled so that computer time could be best utilized. Even so, machine failures in all networks created backlogs over which cataloging departments had little control. And it was not only the large libraries that suffered from downtime and network overload. Catalogers at Sonoma State, the smallest library in the sample group, talked about the continuous frustration of planning work using the OCLC terminal only to confront unexpected telecommunications or maintenance problems that forced continuous revisions of time and production schedules.

Under the manual system, the head of cataloging determined workflow and set production quotas, goals, and standards, working in consultation with other catalogers and other members of the library administration. In the automated system, network computer availability affected scheduling while system analysts and non-cataloging administrators began to exert more influence over setting production standards. The reasons for this emerge from network planning and marketing activities. Basically, network systems were sold to administrators as ways to avoid duplication of cataloging effort, thereby increasing production and decreasing unit costs. In one of its publications, OCLC *Newsletter* (1982:1) proclaims that it provides "More for Less," and " . . . has two fundamental objectives: to increase availability of library resources for users and to reduce the rate of rise of per-unit costs in libraries." These desired results flow naturally from the integrated nature of the bibliographic data base:

With this computerized database, only one library prepares the original catalog entry for an item. . . . Through economy of scale, the OCLC system reduces per-unit costs. . . . Library staff productivity rises, and access to information improves for everyone.

But accepting other libraries' cataloging does not result merely from having it available. After all, cataloging of the Library of Congress and many other libraries had previously been available through the *National Union Catalog*. It results from the willingness of cataloging departments to accept standardized copy and forego local variations or upgrading. In five of the six departments where interviews were held, catalogers expressed the conviction that network participation had helped accelerate an already evident trend among administrators to stress production over quality. They mentioned, as did the administrators at all these institutions, that the cost of network participation (terminals, network and telecommunications charges, etc.) was high and could only be recovered through increased production and/or decreased personnel costs in the cataloging department. Thus administrators participated in networks to lower unit costs and were then almost compelled to follow the recommendations of those networks to accept standardized cataloging in order to pay for their new fixed costs in the network. As one cataloger at San Francisco State noted: "We're watching scenes from a self-fulfilling prophecy; administrators justified networks by saying that they would reduce costs and they're going to make it happen even though it means a big reduction in cataloging quality."

Indeed, there seems to be an almost universal perception among the catalogers that I spoke to that quality has declined because of the emphasis on uncritically accepting contributed copy. This neatly supports the 1976 findings of William Luquire. Luquire studied 25 libraries that were members of the Association of Research Libraries and also participated in OCLC. According to Luquire (1976:347–348):

No matter how good or how poor the basic public image, no matter how prestigious or lacking in prestige the library, the staff at all levels, almost unanimously, stated that they would have to sacrifice "quality" if they were to accept, without major revisions, the OCLC contributed copy.

Luquire comments that he pointed out to the catalogers that it was hard to imagine such a result in all cases since, after all, the high cataloging quality of many prestigious academic libraries was now being made available to smaller institutions who should be able to upgrade their own records as a result. But Luquire could not convince the catalogers of the logic of his position or change their convictions that decline in cataloging quality resulted from network participation. Luquire was really puzzled by the catalogers' attitudes and decided to interview intensively on the quality issue. His conclusions are fascinating because they highlight the problem of defining what cataloging quality really consists of (1976:248):

After extensive questioning in all interview institutions, it appeared that the notion of "quality" was not what was generally meant by the term. Also, the likelihood that high quality cataloging of many large, prestigious libraries, with their sophisticated, subject trained staffs was now available to smaller libraries, seemed to have no effect on this preconceived notion of "sacrificing quality." . . . It was obvious that at some point on the spectrum some of the institutions should begin to gain rather than lose "quality" since the law of averages usually requires it. No real answer was possible or appropriate regarding this apparently psychological perception. One possible explanation is that the notion of "quality" is usually confounded with the notion of adherence to consistency with past cataloging practice.

Certainly my interviews confirmed that catalogers believed that maintaining consistency with past practice was the best way to guarantee present quality. At three libraries, catalogers noted that whereas there had previously been intensive revision by catalogers of each others' work, that practice was now dropped. Although they were actually pleased by this change and did not care for the "Big Brother" aspects of continuous revision, this did not change their belief that revision was one strong pillar of cataloging quality control that had now been knocked away. In like manner, catalogers at Berkeley noted that they used to place their initials on the cataloging card that was placed in the card catalog. Now, when cataloging copy is input into RLIN, the initials are taken off the record. At least one cataloger feels that, "Somehow, try as you will, you are going to be less responsible about that record." At San Francisco State, a cataloger commented at least three times on the elimination of an important quality control check in the serial authority file (a file that establishes the official name of the serial for cataloging purposes). The fact that this same librarian was aware that not one patron had complained about increased difficulty using the serial file did not affect her professional judgment that eliminating a long-standing procedure had to result in declining quality.

Over and over again, catalogers that I spoke to confirmed the loss of quality in the records emanating from their departments. Basically, they attributed this to the perceived decline in professional control over the priorities of the department. Everyone commented on the growing administrative demand for productivity. At San Francisco State, a cataloger mentioned at a group meeting that "Quality control is no longer a concern for any library. It's quantity control that they're after." Everyone present nodded in agreement. And at the University of Washington, a cataloging supervisor told me that the group's unofficial motto had been changed to "Don't strive for perfection."

A very complex shift in values appears to be occurring in the world of cataloging. Catalogers have firmly held conceptions of what a quality product looks like and these views are highly influenced by past training and background. In general, catalogers tend to be people who like to create rules and adhere to them. This characteristic is so prevalent that even the United States Department of Labor Employment Service (1977:19) takes note of it when describing these workers:

INTERESTS

A preference for activities of concrete and organized nature and for situations that are primarily nonsocial in nature.

TEMPERAMENTS

Adaptability to situations involving repetitive work that is carried on according to set procedures and sequences and to situations involving the control and planning of an entire activity.

In the six sample libraries, most catalogers are middle aged (30's–50's) and very few new employees have been added to their work group in recent years. As a result, the six cataloging departments are operating with fairly homogeneous concepts of what high cataloging quality consists of, but with declining capacity to make that quality occur.

On the other hand, the administrators in these libraries are spending increasing amounts of their time thinking about new uses for the computer. Some of them have already developed computerized library catalogs (Stanford and Berkeley). All the others are in the process of planning this new type of cataloging format. These administrators are focused on change and on new approaches to finding material. For them, the cataloger's emphasis on complete description of a cataloged item (e.g. height of a volume, number of illustrations, contents notes, cross references, and checking of authority files for authors' names) and careful check for accuracy is not only costly, it is irrelevant. They feel confident about this attitude because they already have the experience of using network data-base cataloging and have received few patron complaints about its quality. Thus one library administrator at San Francisco State stressed that she is interested in helping the user find material, believes that standardized records in the network data base accomplishes this, and sees no reason to strive for more than that goal. "To be truthful, I'm seeking a definition of minimum standards for a useful catalog, not quality control of a finely tuned catalog."

This statement revives echoes of the long-standing debate about the catalog as a finding tool versus the catalog as an extensive file of linked bibliographic data (bibliographic catalog). But the new element in this debate is the growing conviction among the administrators in the six libraries that catalogers might possess the technical skills to properly edit a record or classify a book, but their training is too narrow, their direct contact with patrons is too infrequent, and their understanding of computer systems and network services is too minimal for them to be able to develop relevant judgments about the best kind of information to be created on the computer. It is true that in every library specific catalogers were cited by administrators as possessing good judgment and interest in developing fine information records. But these statements by administrators were always made in the context of remarks about the need to broaden planning for library catalogs far beyond the ranks of cataloging departments.

Although no administrator at any library even hinted at the idea of deprofessionalizing cataloging, every one of them had, in reality, already begun the process. For all six libraries, the most significant cataloging event of the past decade is the introduction of, or planning for, the online catalog. In Berkeley, the University of California union catalog, MELVYL, was developed by the systemwide planning office, ULAP; at Stanford, the Systems Office developed SOCRATES, the new online catalog. At the other libraries, catalogers play some role on committees developed to create the online catalog but nowhere do their numbers dominate the committee or their personnel set its priorities. In other words, at best catalogers are sharing in the planning process for the online catalog. In none of the libraries are they dominating the process. Even though the administrators that I interviewed felt that catalogers could and must play significant roles in the library planning process, most still supported the view stated by Richard De Gennaro (1981:1040):

Online systems are providing powerful new subject and word capabilities which will increase access to collections and begin to make many of our traditional subject cataloging and classification conventions redundant or obsolete. It remains to be seen whether cataloging, which is already in some disarray, will be able to recover its former preeminence in the library profession or whether it will be further undermined by its inability to respond effectively to a rapidly changing economic and technical environment.

And it is not only administrators who are skeptical about the real value of catalogers' work. At each of the six libraries, catalogers expressed pride in the prevailing sense of professionalism among cataloging librarians and saw this as the only guarantee of continuing quality cataloging. On the other hand, many of these librarians also noted that they were no longer sure that patrons now, or perhaps ever, required this quality. At San Jose a cataloger remarked, "I've never understood why we put so much information on the card. I doubt that it's ever used." At Sonoma State I was told that, "Even catalogers find it hard to explain why AACR2 was implemented. The costs involved in changing the catalog will never be justified by the benefits to patrons." At San Francisco, a librarian who loved being a cataloger, and who proudly paraded visitors to the departmental authority control files, nonetheless felt compelled to say:

Catalogers are beginning to ask the previously unmentionable question—Does any user need a perfect record? If so, what's the cost? Is it worth doing, even at a low cost? Once these questions are brought into the open, there'll be no going back to the good old days of quality control.

At Berkeley, a cataloger noted that whereas catalogers are really interested in upholding standards to meet the requirements of other catalogers, "... now patron access is the buzzword and things are going to change a lot."

Thus it seems that suspicion about the utility of the cataloging function is high, not only among administrators, but within the ranks of catalogers. This psychological undermining of the catalogers' status is further reinforced by shifts in the percentage of total departmental material they are cataloging and in the nature and value of the original cataloging still left under their control.

Since the introduction of network cataloging, library assistants have become responsible for producing the bulk of cataloging in each of the six libraries studied. Each library has different rules for determining which network record can be accepted without revision, which record can be revised by a library assistant or clerk, and which network copy is so flawed that it needs review by a cataloger. Since OCLC is the largest

network, it is not surprising that libraries report the highest
"hit rate" (percentage of searched records found in the data
base) from it. Thus, San Francisco, San Jose, and Sonoma State
cataloging supervisors noted several times during interviews
that up to 98 percent of their departments' total cataloging is
generated by a record found in the OCLC data base. Berkeley,
although a member of RLIN, initiates all searches for cataloging copy through the OCLC data network. The reason it does
so is to take advantage of the high hit rate and so be able to
utilize library assistants, and not catalogers, to create most
new cataloging records. The University of Washington, although linked to WLN by political and organizational ties, also
uses OCLC to search for monograph records, once again because its hit rate makes it possible for library assistants to
locate and process records without much intervention or review
by catalogers. Stanford, the only one of the sample libraries
that exclusively uses RLIN, also has a high hit rate and gen-
erates more than 80 percent of its total cataloging from network
copy processed by library assistants.

The cataloging copy that the library assistants are locating
during their data-base searches describes the most current and
popular books and other library materials. This is the type of
item most quickly processed by the Library of Congress, whose
cataloging all sample libraries accept with little or no revision.
When, for some reason, these items do not receive Library of
Congress cataloging, they are rapidly processed by some library
participant in the network and these records become available
to all other institutions. What all this means is that current
English books, serials, music scores, etc. that are easy to catalog
and/or important, or are in great demand, will quickly receive
some form of network cataloging that can be processed by library assistants in a fairly routine manner. It also means that
newly acquired material that cannot be located on the network
is likely to be chronologically old, or in a foreign language, or
esoteric, or in very low demand. In fact, many of the items that
comprise the original cataloging backlog of the six sample libraries, and most particularly the backlogs of the three large
research libraries, have two or more of these characteristics.

As network data bases expand, library assistants find it easier to locate material and their productivity increases. Nowhere is this shown more dramatically than at Berkeley. In 1982, the Cataloging Department was reorganized into two sections: copy cataloging and original cataloging. Although a professional cataloger is in charge of copy cataloging, the rest of the section consists of library assistants and clerks. The section has received a mandate from the library administration to accept all Library of Congress cataloging and to accept and revise all other cataloging found in the OCLC network provided that it has Library of Congress subject headings and does not differ significantly from the item in hand being cataloged (e.g. the publication date, the edition, or the number of pages are totally different).

In the period since this reorganization, cataloging volume has tripled at Berkeley. An evergrowing backlog of acquisitions has begun to diminish and "hot" items (materials of current interest in great demand) are reaching patrons much more quickly. All these beneficial changes result from library assistant, not cataloger, activities. Another result of those activities is that the cataloger now has left only the most difficult, dated and time-consuming material.

In the past, catalogers usually specialized in subject or language areas, reviewed all the materials acquired in those areas and cataloged both the "hot" items (to get them in circulation quickly) and the difficult ones. This process kept the cataloger knowledgeable about the subject area and thus much better equipped to be able to assign subject headings and classification numbers. Now, 80–98 percent of important current English language material is processed by library assistants. The cataloger has to work in several subject areas because there are not enough items that require original cataloging in most disciplines to warrant subject specialization. Therefore, the professional loses mastery over the literature in a given area. This loss of control and knowledge slows the cataloger. Thus, the catalogers have to exert extra effort just to maintain their previous production statistics.

Working on the material now left in the backlog also requires increased psychological effort. It is sometimes of very limited local interest. Catalogers in the sample libraries often mentioned their suspicion that in many cases only the person who ordered the material would ever read it.

Many of the catalogers that I spoke to feel real distaste for the work left to them. Stanford librarians, for instance, have nicknamed their backlog "the dregs," and other cataloging departments variously call it "the slime," "the uglies," "the dump," and "the leftovers." These names provide a humorous way to highlight a sad reality—in the network environment, the work of original catalogers is certainly becoming less pleasant and is probably less significant, less prestigious, and harder to justify. People working with dregs, slime, and leftovers are not usually held in high esteem within an organization. This reduction in status affects not only the way the organization treats the catalogers, but the way they perceive themselves.

Some of the catalogers that I spoke to conceived of cataloging as a dying or doomed profession. Still others felt that the profession and the rules and standards that it had created were significant, but that most of the work now being performed by individual catalogers could soon be taken over by library assistants. In other words, they conceded that a goodly proportion of traditional cataloging work either had been or would be deprofessionalized. All catalogers expressed awareness of the enhanced status of library assistants, the group most familiar with terminals and network rules and documentation.

The sheer volume of that documentation is staggering. OCLC, for instance, has issued 17 major manuals, each consisting of hundreds of pages of detailed procedures for formatting and inputting records into its system. The level of detail, the breakdown of every rule into several subrules to be implemented in an ordered sequence, the enormous emphasis on punctuation and coding, all provide evidence of organizing network activities and rules around an extremely precise and narrowly focused knowledge base. But, as Wilensky noted in his article on professionalism (1964:148), the distinctive feature of the professional knowledge base is that it occupies the middle ground between the precise and the amorphous, the narrow and the broad focus on a specialized area of learning. Thus network documentation, which is designed to define the precise and narrow software procedures for correctly recording infor-

mation in defined fields in the computerized data base, is likely
to be used most often by clerks and library assistants. In other
words, most network documentation and the activities resulting from that documentation are based on a clerical, not a
professional, knowledge base.

Catalogers mentioned many instances when assistants con-
sulted each other, instead of the professional catalogers in the
library, about the intricacies of cataloging in a network environment. This same issue was touched on with great dismay
on several occasions at the Oglebay Institute on Quality Control (1983:35). Anaclare F. Evans "... noted that clerical and
paraprofessional staff tend to ask their peers for instruction
rather than their supervisors—a form of folklore training—
which sometimes results in increasing internal processing
problems and errors." Given this concern, it is surprising that
at that same Institute (1983:41) Richard Greene, Head of OCLC's
Bibliographic Maintenance section, reported that the network
primarily relied upon library assistants to determine whether
alleged errors reported against catalogers had, in fact, occurred, without provoking much comment or any anger. Yet
this delegation to paraprofessionals of the right to evaluate
professional work is a direct attack upon catalogers' claims to
professional autonomy. Perhaps catalogers have ignored this
overt network attack on their power because of preoccupation
with their declining status in their employing libraries.

It is true that the work of library assistants is controlled by
the schedule of the networks, bounded by network input rules
and remains under the supervision of catalogers. But in all of
the sample libraries, the product of their work is becoming
more important, their knowledge of and access to the computer
is making them more productive, and they are becoming more
valuable to their libraries. Just the opposite phenomenon af-
flicts the catalogers. Decreased subject specialization, combined
with the fact that most catalogers do not directly input material
at the terminal and are therefore not conversant with all technical network requirements, leads to the present situation where
both professionals and catalogers believe that assistants are
usually more knowledgeable about network standards than
catalogers. In the group of sample libraries, the most extreme

example of the shift in importance of the catalogers vis à vis the library assistants is at Berkeley. The cataloging copy group, consisting of one supervising cataloger and 34 library assistants and clerks, is equipped with terminals and printers and has received training (admittedly at a fairly low level) on all four automated cataloging systems being used at the University Library. In addition, as one library assistant disclosed, everyone is aware of the positive attitude of the library administration toward this section. Many outside visitors have been invited to tour through the section and employees have been encouraged to demonstrate their work. When the cataloging copy section produced 5000 records in a month, thus setting a new record, the entire staff was treated to a wine and cheese party by the library administration and the production feat was publicized throughout the library. By contrast, the original cataloging section, composed of 12 catalogers and the equivalent of 2 library assistants, has no computers, no printer, almost no clerical assistance, no training on OCLC, no terminal linking it to MELVYL, the University of California's online catalog, and no evidence of plans for a wine and cheese party.

What the original cataloging section does retain is a belief in its own standards and the need to adhere to them in order to maintain the prestige of its institution. This same sentiment is expressed at Stanford where catalogers note proudly that any Stanford-produced record found in the network data base will immediately be recognized as high-quality work. Yet the irony of their situation is apparent to catalogers in both institutions and to any outside observer. At both these great research libraries the need to process material in a cost-effective and timely manner has impelled administrators to decree that network cataloging copy should be processed with little or no revision. This means that cataloging from hundreds of institutions will be accepted and this material will greatly vary in its quality. On the other hand, material cataloged at Berkeley and Stanford still is subject to stringent quality control standards. As a result, 80–98 percent of the current English language cataloging records in the new online catalogs is being transferred from network data bases and being processed with fairly minimal quality control checks. The remainder of the cataloging—the oldest, least significant, and least used material—is receiving the highest level cataloging and the most expensive quality control review. When all these records are input into the catalog, there is no way for the patron to identify and appreciate the value of the work done by the professional catalogers. Only in the network data base (where records are identified with the inputting library's code) does evidence of the high cataloging quality standards of these research libraries remain.

Thus, as a result of network participation, library catalogers find themselves with diminished ability to control the workflow, the organization, the overall quality standards, and the planning of new services in their work environment. Moreover, the loss of ability to catalog the most important books or those in greatest demand in a subject area greatly undermines the faith of catalogers, and all other library personnel, in the assertion that they are performing significant and useful tasks that have social value within a library context.

Both the literature on professionals and on deprofessionalization emphasize the importance of professional autonomy, the right granted by society to this group of workers to determine the priorities, work procedures, and evaluation processes for the nonroutine, complex, and/or critical work that they perform. In the case of the professional cataloger, the demystifying of the catalogers' knowledge base by outsiders, using new technology, creates a direct attack on the autonomy of the cataloger and supports the process of deprofessionalization. Moreover, while it is certainly true that a small core of catalogers are involved in some important planning committees, evidence from the sample libraries reveals that most catalogers are working with material that lacks significant value for most library patrons. Then too, most of the work previously handled by catalogers is now standardized, made routine, and fragmented into small specialties that can be handled by people with less training. This is precisely the process at large Berkeley and at small Sonoma State. In both cases, library assistants have already become, or are in the process of becoming, subject specialists for network-produced records. (Sonoma State, for instance, employs a Library Assistant 3 [the highest level para-

professional position] to process almost all of its music record-
ings and scores.) As this process continues, distinct boundaries
between paraprofessional and professional become blurred and
the uniqueness of professional tasks disappears.

In her seminal article on deprofessionalization, Toren (1975)
divided professionals into two categories—the humanistic, wel-
fare-oriented professionals (doctors, lawyers, social workers,
nurses, etc.) and the more scientific and technically based
professionals (engineers, accountants, scientific researchers,
etc.). Since catalogers focus on rules, relationships, and organization of information, it is logical to place them in the sci-
entific-technical category. But catalogers are part of the
profession of librarianship and librarians as a group consider
themselves a service, client-oriented profession, motivated by
high ethical standards.

Toren feels that because of the service ideal and ethical code,
professional-client relationships have been governed by the
professional's claim to autonomy (freedom from lay control) and
authority (the duty of the client to obey). But once professional
duties become routine and standardized, clients and employers
begin to assert their own rights to define and assess the proper
role for the professional. One of the striking findings of this
research is the skepticism about the value of the service being
created and defined by catalogers. Not only administrators but
catalogers too are questioning whether patrons really benefit
from many of the rules and standards now in force. Such a
phenomenon matches very closely with Toren's description of
the deprofessionalization of the service oriented professonal
(1975:333–334):

It is not, however, professssional expertise which is primarily called
into question, but rather the prerogatives to decide on goals and to
determine the nature of interaction with others. A possible process of
deprofessionalization is thus indicated in the sense that the derived
attributes of professionalism, i.e. autonomy, authority, monopoly, and
prestige, will be modified and limited to various extents.

Whether judging changes in the cataloger's role from the
perspective of the technical or the humanist professional, the

negative influence of network membership is clear. Networks create an impetus toward the deprofessionalization of the majority of catalogers and, in fact, may prove to be the catalytic agents that trigger reductions in status for professional catalogers.

CHAPTER IV

Social Control

In my review of the literature I cited Zald (1976) as describing social control as a process made up of 4 elements:

1. The formulation and dissemination of standards of performance.
2. The surveillance of performance.
3. The sanctioning or reinforcement of desired behavior.
4. The discovery and punishment of deviance, the failure to comply with established norms.

All institutions develop procedures to control and monitor the work they produce. Library networks, for instance, require participating institutions to sign contracts that obligate them to adhere to network cataloging standards. These contracts always have a clause requiring full members to input all of their original cataloging in acceptable network format. The purpose of this clause is both to enrich the communal data base and to insure that participating libraries are fully committed to the network and willing to integrate their cataloging with it. Such requirements also insure that in time the libraries become dependent upon the networks for important peripheral services such as archival tapes and interlibrary loans, but their primary purpose is to enforce network participation and conformity to their standards. These contractual obligations are very significant and have been honored at all the libraries I examined, even when doing so has incurred considerable extra costs. Thus, although Berkeley and the University of Washington use OCLC to find cataloging, they still input all their original cataloging into their "home" networks (RLIN and WLN respectively) in order to abide by the obligations they have accepted.

At the six sample libraries, network documentation was very visible and catalogers were, in general, aware of the inputting requirements of their networks and the threat to their status as library assistants became increasingly knowledgeable about network rules and standards. However, their most intense discussions centered around the heightened visibility of bibliographic records and the increased monitoring and evaluation of their work that resulted from it. They share this consciousness of heightened visibility with library professionals throughout the United States who often comment on its negative consequences for catalogers. In her report on factors affecting the adoption of OCLC, Markuson (1976:88) identifies one striking development associated with network cataloging visibility—the creation of blacklists, lists of acceptable and unacceptable cataloging departments:

Many libraries are reluctant to accept catalog records from other libraries until they have some "feel" for the care and concern given to inputting and cataloging. Many OCLC users have a list of acceptable and unacceptable libraries in terms of use of OCLC records. The quality of the data base is thus a concern to all users and is an area which OCLC is continually working on.

Susan Martin, Library Director at Johns Hopkins University, expresses the prevailing administrative sentiment that nonstandard records must be identified and eliminated because they create extra costs (1979:213):

We have on our hands millions of "dirty" or "brief" or nonstandard bibliographic records which do not fit easily into the systems we want to use, do not provide for all processing needs, and can be upgraded to full bibliographic format only at great expense.

In a speech at the Oglebay Institute (1982:53), Richard Greene of OCLC felt compelled to defend the reputation of Ohio's Wright

State University catalogers against the bad notices they were receiving as a result of the records input into the data base:

People still tend to point their fingers at Wright State University's records in the Online Union Catalog. Those records were input when there were no established standards, and Wright State has taken a lot of undue flack about them.

At the six libraries where I held interviews, catalogers were aware that their work was nationally visible. At San Jose, two catalogers mentioned that while only 2–3 percent of departmental output was original cataloging, great care needed to be expended on the cataloging copy. When asked if the material was especially significant they said no, that in fact it primarily consisted of campus M.A. theses (work not usually regarded as the most stirring intellectual matter). But in their opinion the honor of the library rode on the quality of the cataloging that thousands of library participants in the network could identify as coming from San Jose. At a meeting of Berkeley catalogers, participants stated that they were not concerned with the evaluations of their cataloging by other libraries because they felt confident about the quality of the work they produced. But some time later in the discussion, there was general group agreement that it was important to produce high-quality records for input into RLIN because Berkeley's national reputation and prestige was at stake. At the University of Washington, a cataloger mentioned that when the library first switched to OCLC, catalogers were astounded by the variation of quality among cataloging departments. For a while some catalogers were so concerned about the judgments others would make of their work that they almost became paralyzed and their production dropped. Since that time, however, "familiarity has bred contempt," and most University of Washington catalogers feel that any objective judgment of their work would inevitably rank them far above the prevailing OCLC norm. Catalogers also expressed the view that seeing other cataloging helps develop insight and judgment about what constitutes a good bibliographic record. In general, they felt that analyzing the cataloging in OCLC was good training for them and usually left

them feeling that their work was being validated. But catalogers in that same library, working in the Serials Department
and using the Washington Library Network (WLN), had an
entirely different perspective. They felt unnerved because being
required to review other institutions' cataloging had convinced
them that there probably was no one right way to interpret
the rules. This perspective is especially interesting because
WLN is the only one of all the networks that revises every
record and prides itself on its consistency. At any rate, Washington University catalogers felt that experience with WLN
made them more flexible, but less certain of the validity of any
professional cataloger's judgment.

If visibility leads to the questioning of previously unchallenged professional assertions of expertise, the compilation of
the error tallies described in Chapter 1 goes one step further
and creates a network-defined system for standardized evaluation of the supposedly unstandardized product of the professional. These error reports are also an oblique challenge to one
of the prime elements in professionalism: the right of the group
to monitor itself and to develop appropriate sanctions and rewards. For catalogers working at OCLC-affiliated institutions
this loss of autonomy is linked to another potentially devas-
tating development—the delegation by the network to its library assistants of the power to evaluate alleged errors in
cataloging and to publicize their ranking of cataloging through
the error tallies.

In discussions with library administrators, it became clear
that they consciously or unconsciously are aware of this direct
threat both to their catalogers' autonomy and to their own
institution's express authority to evaluate employees. In no
institution does the library director become personally involved
in reviewing error tallies, although they are mailed to the
library director's office. Instead, these reports are always dis-
patched to a lower level, usually the head of cataloging, who
is given discretion about how they are to be emphasized and
circulated. Although most catalogers interviewed were aware
of these tallies, almost all of them were far less concerned about
their departmental error rates than they were about the overall
judgments of their departments made by outsiders and based

upon the heightened visibility of their records. They were also aware that their home institutions were not using the tallies in any threatening or even significant ways.

This unanimous avoidance of the error tallies by high-level library administrators may reflect a fairly common type of response by managers. As Rose Coser (1961) pointed out in an article discussing professional-manager relationships, persons high in the hierarchy often deliberately go out of their way to restrict their own observation of subordinates' activities. They do this to mitigate the impact of their own authority and to promote compliance by means of observance of professional norms, rather than through actual inspection of professional activities.

Thus catalogers in the six sample libraries generally expressed confidence that error tallies would not be used by their institutional administrators to initiate punitive actions. Network personnel also emphasized that their procedures were never designed to form the basis for punishing deviant catalogers. At RLIN there is not even a published institutional error tally and the network does not favor creating one. In general, the Quality Assurance Manager relies on the members' high internal standards and their own self-monitoring practices to identify and correct errors. He stresses in his reports and his talks with participating library staff members that cataloging rules change and that errors reported now may have been correct input at the time that the record was created. Moreover, the manager emphasizes that he does not have, nor does he seek, authority to enforce quality control standards because RLIN libraries are committed to high institutional standards and there is really good internal policing of the product going into the data base. That is why RLIN documents use the phrase "should be" instead of "must" when defining standards for each field.

At WLN, error rates are tallied and are the basis for assigning members to Beginning, Intermediate, and Good categories. Since Beginning libraries receive the most intensive review of their work and are therefore most likely to have it returned for correction, the extra work involved, combined with the delay in entering their records into the data base, does in some sense penalize libraries identified as having a high error rate. But even if this is an indirect penalty, it is not discussed in these terms by network personnel. They relate the error rates to a process of useful feedback and customized revision of the network file.

At the Oglebay conference, Richard Greene (1983:43) several times expressed his fears about improper employer understanding of the uses of the error rate and stressed his intention to publicize mitigating circumstances for a high score (low-inputting libraries, with few records in the data base, need only a few discovered records to develop a high error rate; a high proportion of older records by an inputting library usually results in a high error rate; the library could have a variant edition which it properly cataloged and is being charged with an error because LC or the error-reporting library has a different copy in hand, etc.).

At private meetings at the conference, participants reported two instances where the error rate had been used as supporting evidence by library administrators to terminate a professional cataloger's employment. Still, most people present felt that these actions were aberrations and similar firings were not very likely to occur because administrators were either unaware of, or uninterested in, network error statistics and were focused instead on their in-house production and control procedures. Moreover, the view was expressed that it was not in OCLC's interests to develop tallies that were directly threatening to catalogers' status, because they would then respond by withholding original cataloging, the very source of the richness of the data base. They felt that what OCLC was trying to do was win acceptance of the idea that catalogers should attempt to comply with OCLC norms and use the error rate simply to alert themselves to the fact that their current performance might be falling below network requirements. The catalogers pointed out that OCLC staff were always quite eager to explain the meaning of the error rate to administrators and were developing procedures and promotional activities to defuse its negative implications. Thus OCLC regional networks often contact an offending library and give it a chance to correct a faulty record. If it does so within 90 days, no error is charged against it. Explanations of the error rate have appeared in OCLC publications and were the subject of one section of a speech given by Richard Greene to the administrator-dominated OCLC Users Council in 1982 (OCLC. Users Council, 1982). In that speech, Greene stressed that the primary rationale for the error tally was to provide feedback and some retraining for users.

Feedback and retraining are also major justifications for error tallies by the other networks. During the course of an interview, the RLIN Quality Assurance Manager noted that he was preparing a letter to the network coordinator at the one library he had identified as having consistently poor cataloging. He was requesting that the coordinator review network procedures and standards with the offending library and suggest further training.

At WLN, some libraries are judged to be "incorrigible." When this occurs, a reviser is assigned to the offending institution to work closely with the catalogers and " ... to try and turn them around." But if the reviser decides that the library is hopeless, WLN staff will assume the authority to enter the data base and fix its records. It will not, however, complain directly to the head of the library.

Although its error tallies do not result in the kind of direct network reaction that characterizes WLN, only OCLC has developed a quality control standard and guidelines for its proper use that apply not only to catalogers but to administrators. For catalogers, it is a reminder to monitor their own compliance with current network standards; for administrators it is a warning signal that the catalog department may require more training in network procedures, or that it has discovered problems with those procedures that network personnel should be alerted to. In either case, the network has tried to define the use of the standard in a way that benefits the quality of its data base and also avoids directly challenging catalogers' status or administrative control.

Thus it would appear that the networks act to moderate potential conflict between library catalogers and administrators over quality control issues. At the same time, they obviously play an important role in creating, monitoring, and enforcing quality standards.

Although most interviews involved network-professional relationships, certain themes emerged from these discussions that involved two other kinds of relationships: network personnel and administrators; network policy makers and cataloging peer groups.

In the first instance, there is some evidence that administrators are losing or ceding some of their authority over catalogers to networks. I've already noted that in the six libraries all administrators avoided direct use of error tallies. This type of action obviously does not suit the networks, who, after all, invented tallies for some purpose. In fact, both OCLC and WLN staff use the tallies to alert themselves to the need for training and retraining of library staffs and for more intensive review of the offending library's output. This training may possibly produce long-term benefits for the home library, but in the short run it consumes expensive cataloging time and transfers supervision and discretionary use of training time to the network. In like manner, more intensive revision means more corrections and more time devoted by the cataloger to individual bibliographic records.

The intense interest of administrators in reducing costs is a given in every library and was commented upon by almost every cataloger I interviewed. Despite this focus on production, Directors have not intervened to prevent networks from scheduling training sessions or having catalogers revise alleged errors they created in the data base. Moreover, all administrators interviewed stress that emphasis on network production did not require libraries to abandon quality control because the networks establish, monitor, and enforce standards.

This willingness to comply with some network-initiated activities does not mean that all libraries passively agreed to all requests for use of their personnel time by networks. In fact, in this matter there was great variation in the sample group. Stanford makes few errors and those that are discovered are usually for older records, cataloged under different rules. Therefore, very little attempt is made to analyze the error reports. At San Jose and Sonoma State, error reports are mostly ignored because, as one cataloger noted, "People who report other catalogers' errors must have lots of time to while away, and our catalogers don't fall into that category." This means that errors discovered by these catalogers are seldom reported to their network and information about in-house cataloging practice is bypassed by both professionals and administrators. At San Francisco State, the department head does review error reports to get a general feeling for any patterns of error that his department might be falling into. However, he does not directly discuss individual errors with librarians because he feels that this is too threatening and too demeaning to their professional status. Instead, he sends the reports to a para-professional who distributes them to the catalogers. (Once again, the Coser-defined avoidance of direct professional evaluation is apparent.) As yet no one has used the reports to initiate either in-house training or even group discussion of network cataloging practices. At Berkeley, the cataloging department receives error reports from RLIN, OCLC, and GLADIS (the General Library Automated Data Base and Information System, its in-house information system) from library branches and from filing revisers. Serious attention is paid to repeating patterns of errors, but the network data per se rarely initiates training sessions. On the other hand, Berkeley cataloging errors discovered in the RLIN data base are analyzed and either quickly corrected or proved to be correct cataloging because catalogers in the department believe that outsiders using their records should be confident that they are finding high-quality copy. Only at the University of Washington is there a formalized, high priority response to all error tallies. Alleged defective copy is returned to the responsible cataloger for immediate review. The supervisor reports that catalogers receiving many error reports do respond by reviewing network documentation and their error counts usually drop within a short period of time.

Thus it can be seen that the sample libraries run the gamut of reaction to error reports, going from the extreme of total indifference to the other of immediate response. One generalization that applies to all these reactions is that they are triggered by administrators', not network, dictates. Therefore, although the networks appear to have encroached upon the authority of the individual administrator to evaluate work and to enforce compliance with standards, in the six libraries studied, at least, they had neither the power nor the determination to enforce these standards. Thus there is no clear evidence that a dilution or transfer of administrative authority to set standards has actually occurred.

On the other hand, there is at least one area of standard setting where it appears that administrators are beginning to wrest control from network directors and policy makers. Minimum or base level cataloging is being expanded at all three networks because of explicit lobbying by library administrators. At the OCLC Users Council, within the RLG Board of Governors, and at the highest levels of WLN, library managers have been demanding that networks allow greater discretion to individual institutions about the kinds of material they will exempt from full level cataloging. In addition, they have been requesting that the surcharge for nonstandardized cataloging be reduced, thus lessening the penalties assigned by the networks for nonadherence to quality standards. At RLIN, Base Level Cataloging was introduced in 1983, allowing libraries to enter records which only partially conform to network standards. At OCLC, minimal level cataloging has been in effect for several years. At WLN, there is a lower level of cataloging called Interim Records, but unlike the substandard levels in the other two networks, the records in this format are expected to be upgraded. However, ever since the Washington State legislature decreed that WLN must become self-supporting, administrators have lobbied for weakening of quality control activities. In response to their actions, an ad hoc committee, appointed by the State Librarian, has been assigned to develop a Data Base Integrity Survey and make recommendations about quality control standards. Another WLN manager feels that this study is extremely important because participating libraries have always paid lip service to the ideal of a high quality cooperative network, and "... now it's time to see if they're ready to pay the price for it." The prevailing view of WLN staff was that administrators would ultimately support a lowering of network charges achieved by reducing the size of the quality control staff, even if this resulted in many more substandard records.

This interest in nonstandard cataloging seems upon first inspection to be an awfully short-sighted tactic of the library managers. While they would benefit from reduced time to input an original record, the time saved in this way should be more than offset by the extra editing required to upgrade a contributed minimum record. All libraries use a much higher percentage of contributed than original copy, so the number of records to be edited should outstrip the number to be input. Moreover, records can be input by a clerk, but complex editing requires either a library assistant or a professional cataloger, and in both cases they earn more money than clerks. Finally, expanded use of minimal cataloging weakens the collegial nature of the networks. It encourages libraries to ignore communal standards developed to create records that are most useful to the majority of network participants, in order to save time or money for the original inputting library.

What all these calculations ignore is the growing impatience of library administrators with traditional cataloging. Library literature is filled with articles by administrators decrying the high costs and low relative benefits derived from the imposition of AACR2. At the six libraries, almost all the administrators, and even a goodly sample of the catalogers, felt unable to justify the costs of converting to the new cataloging code. The shock of coping with AACR2, combined with their own consuming interest in and experience with planning online catalogs, provided administrators with extra incentive to assert that they, the library planners, knew more about what is needed on a catalog record than their catalogers did. At three of the libraries, therefore, administrators support the option of expanded minimal record cataloging because they plan not only to input their records in this format, but also to accept contributed copy having less detail without any extra editing. In other words, in half this sample the academic library administrators were in favor of reducing the number of data elements and the complex description contained in the bibliographic record for many of the items acquired by their libraries.

Therefore, there is some economic rationale for administrators to support greater use of minimum level cataloging. This rationale, however, does not work for networks except in a very minor way. It is true that minimum records take less storage space and bring income from the inputting library, but these benefits are offset by the fact that little or no authority work is done for minimal level records. This means that a record may be input under a name or title that is not the authoritative form used by the Library of Congress. When LC cataloging becomes available this record will not be bumped because it is filed under a different heading than the LC record. Thus duplicates and/or improper bibliographic descriptions are more likely to result from minimal than from full level cataloging.

More important, the concept of the standardized record, basis of the network online union catalog, and the delivery of peripheral support services like interlibrary loan, is violated. Yet, despite the obvious problems it poses, some form of substandard cataloging has either been accepted or is now being studied by network policy makers and quality assurance managers. Interviews with these managers revealed that they sympathized with the cost-effective emphasis of library administrators, although they did not agree that using minimal records would produce significant cost savings. However, in two interviews the view was expressed that administrators were exercising legitimate countervailing power within these organizations not only because they wished to save costs, but also because they wanted to force network policy makers to devote less time to enforcing internally devised standards and more time to implementing standards that libraries preferred to work with.

At any rate, it is fairly clear that while networks may have assumed partial de facto control over functions that were once exclusively within the realm of library administrators (definition of standards, monitoring of compliance, providing rewards and penalties), they have also recently begun to concede some of their exclusive internal standard-setting authority to those same administrators. At any point in time, one group or the other may have more power or influence, but the cooperative nature of networks provides some insurance against either group becoming totally dominant.

The final set of relationships—network policy makers and peer groups—offers another example of tandem relationships with power shifting back and forth between groups over time.

Evidence has already been presented to demonstrate that networks threaten catalogers' job security. On the other hand, catalogers and network personnel share a commitment to the concept of quality cataloging and willing compliance with national standards, codes, and rules. While the networks have defined their own input rules, their effect on system programming and computer requirements is far less than the combined requirements for adhering to AACR2, LC practice, and MARC. All of these standards, especially AACR2, are creations of cataloging peer groups. When AACR2 was implemented, the cost to the network was staggering because it involved an immense conversion of records. Yet, in general, network personnel did not join library administrators in criticizing and opposing the implementation of the revised cataloging code. According to network quality control personnel who were interviewed, there were three major reasons for this acquiescent stand:

1. AACR2, although admittedly ambiguous in some of its parts, is overall a more consistent and comprehensive cataloging code.

2. AACR2 is both a national and international standard and conversion to it expands the geographic area where network records can be marketed.

3. Networks consider themselves to be in the forefront of the effort to develop a truly national and international bibliographic format. In order to do so, they must have the cooperation and support of catalogers and their peer groups who represent the most knowledgeable indexing experts in the country.

This partnership between cataloging peer groups and the networks is a strong one. After all, it is the original cataloging input into each network that makes its data base unique and desirable. Moreover, catalogers are expert code and standard creators and networks require such codes for their operation. Finally, catalogers and networks both believe that libraries should be inputting detailed records, adhering to standardized codes, and checking authority files not only because such procedures benefit individual libraries, but also because developing a clean national data base is an ethical imperative of workers concerned with the transfer of information. This view was well expressed by Scott Brutjen of the Pittsburgh Regional Library Center, an OCLC affiliated network, when he talked to an audience primarily composed of catalogers (Oglebay, 1983:3):

> ... we form a mutually supporting environment in which there is quality in the data base and quality in the interpersonal relationships and comradeship that we have developed in our networks. ... I am glad that we, OCLC and the (regional) networks, have been able and will be able to continue work on quality at the local and regional level. But now here, at the national level, we are in a position to make, I think, a great leap forward in this most important effort.

All of the networks utilize cataloging advisory groups, either dominated by, or having a strong representation of, catalogers. These groups are extremely important because they are public representations of the collegial nature of the networks. Moreover, it is under their partial guidance that network internal standards and input rules are changed, adopted, or deleted.

Chapter 1 provided a detailed discussion of network attempts to identify master catalogers and directly utilize their services for quality control activities. OCLC has heavily publicized Project Enhance, which designates superior cataloging departments (chosen by network personnel acting on the advice of cataloging peer councils who have analyzed online visible input records) and authorizes them to change flawed records that they identify. (OCLC. *Annual Report*, 1984.) Since libraries will not be paid for this extra work, why should they participate? The answer is that the catalogers are anxious for this extra control and their employing institutions are receptive to the public status that it accords. As one cataloger member of a peer council noted (Oglebay, 1983:124):

> At a Peer Council meeting the names were passed around and we were asked to decide who would be good people to select. Nothing makes people happier than to call them an expert, so we got a lot of positive response from the people that we asked to participate.

And Richard Greene, Head of Bibliographic Maintenance at OCLC, stressed another tempting reason for becoming a de

facto network reviser (Oglebay, 1983:43): "Deleting [substand-
ard] records is a very high priority. That is one thing that
everyone likes to do; it means power."

At WLN, quality control personnel viewed their network's
relationship with its cataloging advisory group, the Bibliographic Standards Committee, as one based on a shared moral
perspective. Thus they spoke of the committee as a "good dedicated group," which sometimes suffered from "a lapse from
grace," but was basically committed to high professional standards. In like manner, WLN is preparing to select master cataloging departments who will be subject to only periodic revision
of their records and will be placed in a "Superior" category,
once again a public designation both of quality and rank within
the library profession.

Thus in many ways the relationship of networks and catalogers is far more collegial than the relationship of catalogers
and administrators, or the relationship of administrators to
networks. Therefore, although there is evidence of network
actions and policies that satisfy all the criteria for proving that
quality control of cataloging is developing into social control
of catalogers (standard setting, surveillance of performance,
sanctions and reinforcement of behavior, the discovery and
punishment of deviance), it is in part counterbalanced by the
success of cataloger peer groups in becoming part of the network standards definition process. Change has certainly occurred in the balance of power between networks and
administrators, between administrators and catalogers, and
between networks and peer groups. In general, the shifts have
produced negative consequences for most catalogers and, at
least in the sense of autonomy on the job, these professionals
have become subject to more social control by administrators
and by networks. On the other hand, the power of cataloger
peer groups appears to be growing and greatly influencing the
course of network development. Although the peer groups comprise a small fraction of cataloging professionals, their importance and expertise guarantees catalogers continued access to
the decision-making process of networks. Network decisions in
turn affect individual libraries and the power relationships
between the various professional, technical, and administra-

tive groups they employ. One of the great ironies this case study discloses is that networks, catalytic agents for the deprofessionalization of cataloging, are also among the staunchest defenders of catalogers' codes, status, and expertise. As yet, neither catalogers nor networks have attempted to confront or rationalize these contradictory roles; perhaps wisely so. Avoidance of these areas of conflict permits both interested groups to work together and increase their power vis-à-vis individual libraries and their administrators.

CHAPTER V

Peer Groups

In the preceding chapter, the dynamics of cataloger-administrator and cataloger–network personnel relationships were explored. The differing scenarios and shifting alliances of administrators and network personnel vis-à-vis catalogers are, in some sense, predictable since these different occupational groups would be expected to define and rank cataloging priorities in terms of their own perspectives, priorities, and goals. Far more surprising is the intensity of the relationships that catalogers have developed within their own ranks as a result of network visibility and participation.

In my survey of the literature on catalogers as professionals, constant reference was made to catalogers' interest in developing perfect records which could be evaluated and appreciated by their peers. In the sample libraries, catalogers who were interviewed unanimously confirmed the idea that they were concerned with attaining perfect records. Their pursuit of this ideal appeared to include the patron only tangentially. At Stanford, a cataloger mentioned that the quality of the work being produced was insured by the high communal standards of the catalogers and their concern for the prestige of their library among other librarians. Although patrons were not specifically excluded as objects of concern, they were obviously not in the forefront of the catalogers' interests. Patron access problems were rarely referred to.

At San Francisco State, I was told that patrons don't care about quality, but catalogers do. This did not mean that ca-

talogers were indifferent to patrons. Indeed, it was asserted
that they understood client long-term research needs far better
than the average patron and planned accordingly. Like all specialists, catalogers needed to consult with each other in order
to provide responsible services to patrons.

At Berkeley, catalogers acknowledged that they were strongly
aware of colleagues' in-house evaluation of their work and
agreed that perhaps more interest in patron access problems
would be helpful. In fact, the library committee on Bibliographic Control, which was interdepartmental in its organization, would be considering issues of patron access. While this
committee was important, however, catalogers felt that issues
relating to cataloging standards and items placed on the record
would still have to be reserved for the Cataloging Council,
composed strictly of cataloging colleagues, because the present
rules are so complex and intricate that "... no one but catalogers can talk intelligently about these matters."

At every institution, a phrase like "of course catalogers are
perfectionists," "catalogers can't compromise their standards,"
"catalogers catalog for each other because we're the only ones
who understand the importance of the record," was included
in the conversation both as explanation for the decline in catalogers' status in a production-oriented world, and as affir-
mation of the special virtue of the cataloger.

Another reason for the inward focus of these catalogers
emerges from their own work patterns and definitions of expertise. At every library, the catalogers, even the subject specialists, had extremely limited contact with students and with
faculty. They tended to work alone in partitioned alcoves so
that they could devote intense attention to the literature that
they were describing. Lunches and coffee breaks were usually
taken with colleagues within the department or within the
library. Since their contact with their subject areas rarely was
the result of discussion with practitioners, the catalogers were
isolated from the nonlibrary sources that possessed the subject
expertise to critique and evaluate their work. Whether this
situation resulted from the choice of the cataloger, the indifference of the faculty researcher, or a combination of both was

hard to determine. Perhaps the catalogers felt intimidated by the greater subject expertise of faculty members and/or suspected that these faculty members lacked interest in the catalogers' unchallenged specialty, descriptive cataloging of the physical characteristics of an acquired item (e.g. number of volumes, edition, translator, etc.). Whatever the cause, the fact remains that since most of the catalogers interviewed were isolated from users, especially knowledgeable faculty members, their only sources for evaluating their work were the cataloging rules and the approval of other catalogers.

In an isolated work environment network visibility can provide potential benefits for catalogers who feel proud of their work and seek to enlarge the audience that is able to appreciate it. Many catalogers in the sample libraries, especially the three large research libraries, fall into this category. Thus Berkeley catalogers bemoan the fact that their initials are removed from the bibliographic record before it is input into RLIN. True, their quality work is still identified as a Berkeley product, but their individual contributions to their institution's prestige will not be known to other catalogers. At the University of Washington, catalogers attempted to compensate for the fact that library assistants cataloged most current material by requiring those assistants to attend weekly catalog department meetings in order to report on changes in the literature or in current Library of Congress practice that they noted. In this way, catalogers could at least maintain second-hand currency with the literature in order to develop the high-quality original cataloging that would be input either into OCLC or WLN and identified as a University of Washington product.

Evidence of the pride of catalogers in their work, and of their quest for each others' approval, sometimes appears in the library literature. Kallenbach and Jacobson (1980: 266), for instance, discuss reasons why the University of Pennsylvania libraries decided to leave OCLC and join RLG/RLIN. Basically, the decision was made at the administrative level that joining RLG would provide a more complete range of services to the University of Pennsylvania's research-oriented patrons. The catalog department supported the changeover for different reasons, however. In RLIN the record of each library can be displayed, whereas in OCLC only the master record appears upon the screen. Thus (1980:266):

> The most notable enhancement for cataloging staff members is the capability for online access to our own cataloging records. Original cataloging, once a source of pride to professional catalogers, can once again be viewed by a larger audience, not hidden in the hexadecimal logic of the library's archive tape.

And a survey of the impact of OCLC on cataloging departments done by Allison and Allen (1979:16) concluded that one of the most valuable benefits of OCLC was the provision of regular opportunities for catalogers to meet and confer with each other under the auspices of the network Cataloging Advisory Committee.

In Chapters 1 and 4, awareness by catalogers of the potential negative effects of visibility was discussed. Scherba and others were cited for discussing the growing number of library blacklists of institutions whose cataloging was deemed to be unacceptable. Greene mentioned the sad fate of Ohio's Wright State University catalogers and their unjustified notoriety for low cataloging standards. At the sample libraries, catalogers were aware of the blacklists and some departments even admitted to creating them, although some fear was expressed that public admissions of this sort of activity might be misinterpreted as libelous actions perpetrated by their departments. On the other hand, all of the libraries had developed some kind of white list over the course of time—lists of libraries whose cataloging could be accepted with little or no revision or of libraries that were especially esteemed for some area of specialized cataloging (e.g. music scores). Although catalogers interviewed had not actually compared their lists with colleagues in other institutions, most felt confident that the same names would appear on the majority of library white lists. A participant at the Oglebay Conference described the process whereby catalogers identify each other, highlight master work, and integrate it into their own institution's catalog (1983:106):

Users groups [cataloging libraries who participate in network committees] have an unwritten peer council for quality control. One way they have done this is to provide you a chance to meet your peers in other institutions. You learn what their symbols are so you know whose work you are looking at. Now this is an informal way, but it creates an atmosphere wherein peer pressure can be quite effective. Certainly I now look for certain institutions because I know that I am going to be able to accept their work and find it of higher quality than I will of other institutions. I also can almost bet that if I wait a week, in some instances, certain institutions will have input the record that I am looking for, if I'm really not willing to commit myself on a given title.

Thus specialists seek out each other and an informal rank of master cataloger appears to emerge as a result of network participation. In some instances, it seems that this process is already being refined and formalized. At Oglebay, Richard P. Smiraglia (1983:115) described how music librarians have voluntarily created a group composed of 12 master music cataloging departments, each of which analyzes, describes, and enters into the network material for four bibliographic records monthly. These records are then utilized by other music librarians who are assured that they are of high quality. This program is unfunded and coordinated entirely by cataloger volunteers interested in guaranteeing the development of excellent music bibliographic records that can be used nationwide.

The white lists also make it easy to create spinoff products. Because OCLC, its regional networks, and its cataloging advisory groups know where the high-quality cataloging departments are located, they are now both confident in, and capable of, assigning these departments the task of revising errors in the data base. As noted in Chapter 1, Project Enhance, inaugurated in December 1983, with its designation of 20 revising libraries, is a direct offspring of network visibility, quality control, and evaluation. In like manner, the OCLC Western buddy system relies on identifying master catalogers who will volunteer their services to review the files of new or errant libraries and suggest ways to improve their work.

Finally, both the OCLC regional networks and WLN have compiled resource lists of catalogers knowledgeable both about cataloging rules and network procedures. These lists are available to institutions seeking expert consultants. Of course, the lists also provide the source from which new members of network advisory committees can be drawn.

It is true that acknowledged nationwide cataloging experts existed in the library profession prior to networks. They were usually identified because of their rank (e.g. heads of cataloging departments of major research libraries), their articles in the library literature, or their membership in important state or national cataloging committees. These same factors are still important in identifying cataloging experts, but network participation has added two new possibilities for nationwide renown—participation in network committees and/or quality of cataloging prepared by the individual or the department that he/she represents. In some ways the first of the new possibilities is simply a variation on the old requirements for approval by the establishment. After all, being head of a catalog department, being selected to publish in refereed library journals, or being appointed to national committees, is a function of the cataloger's ability to meet the standards of the existing power structure of the library world. The second of the new paths to cataloging stardom, however, does not fit comfortably into the traditional mold. It stresses performance and peer evaluation rather than administrative approval and political alliances. While this phenomenon is much too new to be realistically assessed, interviews with catalogers reveal a great interest in, and approval of, working peers, especially those that are associated with the networks. In fact, among the catalogers interviewed there appeared to be a high level of consensus that peer group representatives are, as one Oglebay Conference speaker stressed, worthy leaders who have publicly proved their high ethical standards by adhering to high-quality professional cataloging standards, even when doing so sometimes becomes unpleasant (1983:4): "Quality conrol is a lot like cleaning a cat box. It is expected—that is your fellow librarians expect you to keep their data base clean."

But, of course, people who clean out cat litter boxes sometimes develop such strong aversions to their contents that they decide to get rid of the animals responsible for producing the mess. Discussions with network quality control personnel indicate that master catalogers are characterized both by the high quality of their work and their tendency to report substandard cataloging done by others. At Oglebay, real anger was expressed by master catalogers toward perceived polluters of the data base. It was suggested that error-prone catalog departments (1983:107) "... have the duty to seek the guidance of someone who does have the expertise in bibliographic control." In private conversations at Oglebay the view was expressed that OCLC management should develop the courage to unplug the terminals of unworthy libraries. Thus, error reporting is one way that OCLC regional networks identify resource people and potential members of their advisory groups (Oglebay, 1983:4–26). These networks analyze the error reports sent to them, examine the documentation that accompanies the report in order to establish that the record is indeed in error, and develop files of individuals dedicated to maintaining a "clean" data base. The regional networks then review online the work produced by each cataloger and if that work is ranked superior, the error-spotting cataloger will begin to be invited to participate in network committees. In time, this participation will often lead to invitations to join nationwide cataloging advisory committees.

While this process is favorable for the error reporter, what impact does it have on the individuals or departments that errors are assessed against? In general, among the sample libraries, catalogers in the three research institutions were more likely to view the errors as a blow to departmental prestige and to contest the judgment call, despite the fact that administrators in these libraries conformed to the trend noted in Chapter 1 and tended to avoid directly confronting catalogers with this alleged evidence of their mistakes. What worried the catalogers was the effect the tallies might have on the opinion of colleagues in other institutions. These larger cataloging units were also able to react because they had sufficient manpower to devote time to rebuttal. However, even in the three other libraries, some resentment at errors assigned the institution was expressed and, in at least one of them, serious effort was made to review the record and determine if substandard cataloging had actually occurred.

It was only when speaking to network quality control personnel, however, that the rage of the embattled cataloger against whom errors were assessed could be discerned. At all three networks, quality control personnel expressed some feelings of stress resulting from having to deal with librarians whose records allegedly contained errors. Some of the catalogers felt personally compelled to develop huge and thoroughly indexed documentation justifying their innocence. If, despite these protests, their records were revised at the network office, they took personal affront at what they considered to be stains on their professional record. In one of the networks, the strain of dealing with this small, but outraged and vocal, constituency took a noticeable toll upon the entire quality control staff. Network administrators became so concerned that they ordered that group members use some company time to take classes in biofeedback and thus relieve their stress. Unfortunately, this enlightened management strategy was not totally successful. Several biofeedback students experienced additional stress worrying that their bosses would monitor their biofeedback performance and find them at fault for not having relaxed enough. Thus visibility doth make victims of us all!

At another network, the chief reviser separated catalogers into two groups—"those that want to dance and those that want to fence." The dancers are willing to accept revisions for the sake of the consistency of the network data base. The fencers, usually the more renowned catalogers, are supremely confident of their own judgments and will contest every error call. The network reviser (obviously a natural-born fencer) enjoys the contest, admires the combatants, and often makes mental notes that they possess the right stuff needed to become members of network committees.

All of the network quality control personnel commented on what they consider to be a statistically insignificant but fascinating aberration—some catalogers, aware of the visibility and publicity that network participation creates, are deliberately using error reports to disparage the work of colleagues in other institutions. They do this by searching for the records of these colleagues and reporting even the most minute typographical errors that they can discover. Sometimes it is one individual seeking to score against another. Other instances relate to the hostility of competing cataloging departments, especially in institutions that have had traditional rivalries with each other. In this case, technology has made it possible for a new form of the Super Bowl to be played on video screens by competing catalog departments.

But, in general, maintaining standards is not a game to catalogers. It is serious and important work. One of the most striking impressions that emerges from reviewing cataloging literature is the judgmental and moral world view of catalogers, especially in the area of standard setting and enforcement. Previously noted comments in this study include remarks such as "born again catalogers," persons needing "guidance," and "incorrigible cataloging departments" not only because they are colorful, but because they are so plentiful in the cataloging literature. Moreover, during the course of the interviews phrases like "lapses from grace," "worthy peers," and "superior catalogers" appeared to form natural parts of the catalogers' vocabulary—an in-group tone and use of language that an outsider would be more likely to associate with the ministry than with the technical experts catalogers pride themselves on being.

Because they are engaged in protecting the purity of cataloging standards, the emerging subgroups of master catalogers and cataloging peer groups appear to have, quite unconsciously, cloaked themselves in the mantle of the righteous. Like any group of the Elect they are sometimes disliked and resented, but no serious collegial challenge to their right to discover and assign error has yet emerged. In fact, network designation as resource consultants, as approved revisers (e.g. Project Enhance), as "Buddies" for new or wayward cataloging departments, provides new cataloging peer groups with nationwide influence, power, and prestige. This same combination of factors then makes it possible for those groups to pressure networks for the retention of standards and the very detailed records so dear to catalogers' hearts.

This enhanced status is, of course, bestowed on a very small minority of catalogers through network participation. The vast majority of these librarians are threatened by the many de-professionalizing trends that these networks create. Despite this, many catalogers that were interviewed expressed more hope for the survival of their professional ideals as a result of the work of peer groups than through the continued activities of their individual departments. Although sympathetic to pressures placed on the administrative heads of their departments by library directors seeking to reduce costs, they were also fatalistic about the inevitable reduction in quality that these pressures would produce. In like manner, they stoically noted their decline in status within their departments vis à vis library assistants.

In two of the libraries, comment was made about networks providing a new opportunity and a new forum to discuss standards. Moreover, as one San Francisco State cataloger noted, "... networks might be worrisome because they assign errors, but at least they have some interest in discovering them. Most libraries don't care anymore."

In "The Professionalization of Everyone?" Wilensky points out that the optimal knowledge base for professionals is (1964:148) "... neither too vague nor too precise, too broad or too narrow." Cataloging work may well fall into the too narrow and too precise category which is susceptible to being broken into ever smaller components that can then be taught to workers with lesser skills. Wilensky comments that this type of work (1964:149) "... is ripe for elimination by programming on a computer." The deprofessionalization process seems to provide an almost perfect empirical verification of the Wilensky theory. On the other hand, Wilensky also argues that (1964:139)

... many of us might construct a homemade bookcase, few would forego a clergyman at the grave. The key difference is that the clergy's tasks and tools, unlike the carpenter's, belong to the realm of the sacred—which reinforces a jurisdictional claim grounded in formal training and indoctrination. Occupations which successfully identify themselves with the sacred may achieve as much of a mandate by monopoly as those that identify themselves with science.

Thus he charts many paths used by occupational groups in their ascent to the peak of professionalism. At present, there is certainly no evidence that catalogers are consciously trying to replace a diminished knowledge base with an expanded claim to moral superiority. Indeed, striving toward some abstract ideal has always characterized these professionals and turned them inward in a search for collegial approval. But with the rise of designated master workers and knowledgeable peer groups, catalogers appear to be developing a breed of colleagues whose knowledge base is expanding to include an overview of network systems and whose standard-setting influence is acknowledged by network personnel as well as by other catalogers. These workers could possibly develop into new hybrid catalogers, possessing some measure of automation expertise, political clout, and devotion to traditional cataloging standards. If so, there is a slight chance that they are harbingers of the reprofessionalization of cataloging. Thus while the network has sowed the seeds for the deprofessionalization of cataloging, it has also reaped the crop of the new breed of super catalogers. These professionals base their power both on knowledge of network procedures and on the moral purity of their devotion to high standards of cataloging work. Since quality control is the banner under which they all rally, these cataloging masters and peer groups show some evidence of becoming a natural focus for the moral drive and professional aspirations of catalogers. Networks are already becoming aware of the political influence that these groups may possess. Richard Greene of OCLC discussed at Oglebay his concern about (1983:63) "raising sensitivity to the power that these people have, the realization of what they can do to a record and for other users." And WLN staff feel confident that they can discuss policy issues with the cataloger-dominated Bibliographic Standards Committee because "they are strong, solid professionals and know a lot about network standards." Only at RLG/RLIN is the Technical Services/Systems Committee (the primary cataloging advisory committee) chaired and controlled by a library director rather than a cataloger. As Susan Martin (1982:105) noted in her dissertation about network governance, the decision to make the Chair a Director instead of a member of an expert peer group was an early policy decision of RLG designed to insure consideration of the broad needs of the consortium in each major committee. Of course, such a decision also implies that the RLG executive fears that professional, rather than consortium, goals would dominate RLG unless preventive action is taken.

It remains to be seen whether over time peer groups can retain leadership positions in networks and broaden their professional cataloging knowledge base. One positive support for this point of view is that networks conform fairly closely to the kinds of professional organizations described by Bucher and Stelling (1980) and discussed in the literature review. It should be remembered that these organizations foster the development of peer groups concerned with creating, monitoring, and enforcing standards. They also provide a support system to aid professionals to develop new programs that reflect their ethical and service ideals. Finally, they sometimes create a framework for the mediation of potentially conflicting interests, thus making it possible for differing power blocs to work out compromises in a new organizational environment. These actions provide evidence that over time networks could mediate conflict between administrators and catalogers and also help enhance the status of cataloging peer groups.

CHAPTER VI

Quality Control Standards

In the previous chapters, cited interviews and material from the library literature indicated that administrators, network personnel, and catalogers have differing standards for a quality bibliographic record. The evidence presented illustrates that they are positioned at various stages along a continuum, with the majority of catalogers located at one extreme, stressing adherence to every cataloging rule and generally approving of very detailed records that often elaborately describe the physical attributes of the cataloged item and/or its contents. Positioned somewhere near this group are the master catalogers and cataloging supervisors, who are also committed to following cataloging rules, but who emphasize a standardized record over local embellishments. They focus on developing descriptions that contain all required access fields needed to locate the record in the network data base. The distinguishing characteristic of these cataloging professionals is that their concept of quality cataloging embraces network requirements as well as cataloging rules, and network storage, programming, and pricing policies are considered when trying to develop standards that link network activities to cataloging requirements.

Further down the continuum are network personnel, many of whom have been trained as professional catalogers, and all of whom recognize the central importance of the cataloging data base for all network services. Despite this, their primary focus is on network data base organization and on the systems that most economically link bibliographic records and provide

access to them. Because the data base is the primary responsibility and interest of network workers, their emphasis is on
developing computer programs and creating records that can
be utilized for a variety of purposes by a large number of libraries with minimal, or no, revision. At the same time, they
are also concerned about controlling the size of the records
because detailed description that is not of interest to most libraries increases the storage requirements of the networks
without generating the additional income needed to pay for the
extra computer memory that is required.

Finally, library administrators can be discerned stationed in
various locations between network personnel and the farthest
extreme from catalogers—the place where proponents of minimal cataloging reside. To some extent, the cataloging stance
of academic library administrators is affected by the audience
their library serves—-researchers, graduate students, faculty,
undergraduates, etc. It is also largely conditioned by the resources available to the administrators and the demands for
services that they are encountering. In the case of the six sample libraries, those resources have been declining at the same
time that technology has greatly expanded the types of services
that the administrator is expected to provide (e.g. automated
circulation, online reference services, computerized interlibrary loan services). Given this situation, these library administrators, along with most administrators publishing in the
library literature, naturally tend to add a cost-benefit dimension to the definition of a quality record. In other words, quality
is not primarily defined by adherence to the rules but by production of a high volume of records adequate enough to locate
desired items for a patron in a timely manner. Less emphasis
is placed on the record as a bibliographic tool and more on it
as a finding tool. Of course, since administrators are also concerned with utilizing all the network product spinoffs, there is
a high degree of concern that the network bibliographic record
contain enough information that it can be immediately identified as the proper description for the material that the library
is interested in. Once again, there is a cost dimension to this
concern. Standardized records can be manipulated by library

assistants and clerks, rather than catalogers, and are therefore more economical to produce.

The clearest perspective of catalogers' standard-setting activities emerges from an analysis of their attempts to develop national and international codes. This process appears to focus on the inner coherence and completeness of the catalogers' systems, with only peripheral attention to how those systems are utilized by the patron or how the costs involved affect their libraries. Thus the debate on the rationale for AACR2 has always centered around technical considerations that result in providing the cataloger with more consistent guidelines for his/her work. In this regard, AACR2 was created by the very same standard that produced AACR1 in 1967. That standard was proclaimed by Wyllis E. Wright, Chair of the American Library Association Code Revision Committee, who exhorted the committee members to do their work by concentrating on the internal consistency of the code and ignoring any consideration of the costs involved in implementing the revision (Kelm, 1978:22).

The anger and hostility expressed by administrators at the cost of implementing the changes required by AACR2 have already been discussed in some detail in this book. Whatever the merit of these views, it is still undeniable that cataloger-developed codes created the foundation and basic structure for almost all current national and international bibliographic communication and activity. AACR2 was developed by an international catalog advisory committee. Many of its detailed rules are based on the International Standard Bibliographic Description (ISBD), created in 1974 under the auspices of the International Federation of Library Associations and Institutions (IFLA). What ISBD accomplished was to free catalogers from the tradition of using the title page as the primary source of cataloging data. It provided them with a new format that standardized national practices relating to the content and arrangement of a bibliographic record and laid the groundwork for computer manipulation of the standardized data elements in that record. Another cataloging code, MARC, developed explicit standards for a machine-readable format for the ISBD defined print and nonprint data elements, described under AACR2 rules. Thus the standardized description, punctuation, and rules required by libraries and networks in order to communicate bibliographic information to each other in machine-readable format, have all resulted from the cooperative activity of cataloging committees.

Since its creation in the late 1960's, MARC has gone through a revision process and has emerged as MARC II. Catalogers, especially master catalogers, lavish much attention on it (and on its international offspring, UNIMARC) because they see it as the vehicle for producing a computerized international exchange network for bibliographic records. In principle, once this network is in place, using standardized MARC formats, participating libraries could locate and access each others' materials without needing to know the language that the bibliographic record uses. There are three components to the MARC II and UNIMARC records (Hagler and Simmons, 1982:142–147; MARC Formats, 1980–):

1. The arrangement of the record on the magnetic tape so that the computer is able to instantly locate various types of information. This physical arrangement is also the result of standard setting by an international cataloging committee. The standard produced is known as ISO DIS 2709–1973 of the International Organization for Standardization (ISO).

2. The content designators. These special characters and codes identify what the information recorded on the tape relates to (i.e. does the information describe an author, subject, or title?).

3. The cataloging data. This is now described under the international code, AACR2.

Over time, the full MARC record has become more detailed and more complex. Creating such a complex record requires extra effort and time from the professional cataloger (National Library of Canada, 1974) and creates economic burdens for libraries and networks by increasing unit cataloging costs and storage requirements. As yet, few foreign countries have converted to the full UNIMARC standard or to AACR2 because the cost of upgrading their records to these standards is so high.

Moreover, there simply is no conclusive evidence in the library
literature to prove that the use of MARC does result in greater
international exchange of library materials. Despite this, the
cataloging literature, many of the catalogers in the sample
libraries, and most of the catalogers at the Oglebay Quality
Control Institute support the development and use of the full
MARC record because they are convinced that it will ultimately
provide the mechanism for the national and international exchange of information. The point that the catalogers are making is that their standards provide rational guidelines that are
global in conception and that will ultimately benefit all users
because catalogers nationally and internationally can work
with them. Thus, although their focus is on their own standards
and activities, the ultimate beneficiaries of their standard-setting and monitoring activities will be all users of information.
This is the dream and the ideal of catalogers at Berkeley, Stanford, Sonoma State, San Francisco State, San Jose State, and
the University of Washington. Because of it, they share a dedication to creating a national and international bibliographic
language and all approve heartily of the efforts of cataloging
advisory groups to develop this cataloging lingua franca. In
like manner, in its final program document, the National Commission on Libraries and Information Science (NCLIS) stresses
the importance of anticipating information requirements and
developing standards for them. If not, America will face "... a
form of information chaos" for years to come (United States
National Commission on Libraries and Information Science,
1975:52). And in the cataloging literature, discussion of the
idea of Universal Bibliographic Control, the concept of cataloging all material in its country of origin and sharing the
record worldwide, has become accepted as one of the great goals
of the cataloging profession (Chaplin, 1975). Thus the communal energies of catalogers appear to be concentrated on developing cataloging and machine-readable standards that can
be utilized nationwide and worldwide by fellow professionals.
And so, from the catalogers' perspective, quality standards and
quality controls emanate from the work of cataloging advisory
committees, are based on deliberate judgments of professionals
consulting with each other, and result in official pronounce-

ments over time about the amount and format of information suitable for library users.

Network personnel are also concerned with national and international standards. All of the networks are greatly affected by major changes in the cataloging rules or of MARC. The conversion to AACR2 involved huge costs for RLIN, WLN, and OCLC, all of whom had to convert millions of records and reprogram some of their input procedures in order to accommodate changes in the cataloging code. (In fact, OCLC managers became so alarmed about the cost of code changes that they even threatened not to implement AACR2 [Georgia Brown, 1981].) On the other hand, it is clear that conversion to AACR2 could not have occurred as quickly or as completely if networking had not become so entrenched among academic libraries. Thus, while networks bore many of the conversion costs, they also strengthened their claims to being the only adequate, flexible, and timely source of cataloging copy for libraries. In its system description (March 1981), Washington Library Network emphasizes the ease with which changes and revisions are accommodated and stresses that "...the links among the WLN files provide the capability to automatically update all bibliographic records to display the current form of a linked authority heading that has been changed." RLIN and OCLC also have online authority files that make it possible to easily check changes in official forms of names and headings used in cataloging. All networks are developing online systems and software to automatically check input records against cataloging standards and to highlight discovered errors. As yet, no automatic system is capable of making the judgments or the choices between alternative interpretations of a rule that characterize the human revisers in all network quality control departments, but the fact that all these departments foresee much greater computer programmed revision indicates a strong possibility that automated revision of cataloging will ultimately become part of the services offered by networks. At any rate, when network personnel evaluate cataloging standards, they do so both in terms of the internal consistency of the cataloging codes and the impact these codes will have on their existing computer system, their costs, and their relationships to customers. Unlike libraries, where almost every code change or enhancement results in increased short-term costs with almost no offsetting revenues, networks experience negative and positive effects from these changes. True, there are huge reprogramming costs, but the increased rate of code revision makes library use of networks not only desirable, but practically mandatory. Network managers are also aware that they could not have developed their files without MARC and that the incredibly expensive and time-consuming effort to develop MARC II and UNIMARC has also been borne by the Library of Congress and other library agencies. Thus Kilgour, founder of OCLC, in his article on international networks and public policy (1983:243), extolls the support that the Library of Congress has given to networks through its work on codes and standards.

Since the development of national and international standards makes it possible for networks to market their services internationally, they can anticipate potential benefits from the standard-setting activities of catalogers *provided* that some measure of network control can be inserted into the decision-making process that results in the development of new standards, or the revision of old rules. At Oglebay (1983:49–50), Richard Greene reviewed the long list of national and international committees that OCLC and the other networks participate in and discussed the process that takes place within these committees when evaluating a proposed revision or cataloging standard:

OCLC is involved in the review of proposals to change the MARC format. The MARC format document is issued by the Library of Congress; any proposal to change the format, to create a new format, whatever, go through a committee called MARBI an ALA [American Library Association] inter-divisional committee with members from three divisions [cataloging sections of ALA]. . . . All of the bibliographic cooperatives are invited to send representatives, but because it is an ALA committee the bibliographic cooperatives do not have a vote on the committee. However, since they are invited to attend the meetings, they have a lot of voice. For the last four years there have been no voting representatives on MARBI from any of the bibliographic cooperatives but, at this time, there is one, me. We review each proposal in terms of how we can implement it, is it justified in this format, will our users need it, and do they want it. In terms of how we can implement, it sometimes comes down to how much is it going to cost and is it worth the cost. There was a proposal that seemed to be sailing through MARBI and when looked at more closely by RLG and OCLC, we both came up with the same conclusion that this would be a multi-year, multi-million implementation project. The proposal was not passed.

The impact of the networks on the standard-setting process appears most strongly in the areas of developing machine-readable standards and in bringing cost, time, and machine capability considerations into the standard-setting process. In other words, a quality standard or control is evaluated not only for internal consistency but also to determine "how much is it going to cost and is it worth the cost." In January 1983, the OCLC Pricing Committee prepared a five-year plan which emphasized over and over again the bottom line considerations that affect network activities (OCLC. Pricing Committee, 1983):

A significant but little understood, or recognized, cost is to maintain and make available the millions of records in the database. It must be recognized that, regardless of the input or output medium or format, this cost remains and must be covered.

As Richard Greene noted, both RLG and OCLC are concerned with the machine and human costs required to adhere to cataloging codes and they attempt to bring these factors to the attention of catalog standard-setting committees. Since Washington State no longer subsidizes WLN, that network has naturally become more concerned about pricing and the cost of developing and enforcing its own quality control standards. In fact, its recent organization of a marketing review program and its Data Base Integrity Study are responses by the network to the need to discover what quality control is costing the network and if customers think it is worth it.

Do customers think that quality standard setting and enforcement is worthwhile and does the extra effort devoted to enforcing standards produce a payoff for the networks by attracting more business? Judging simply from the sample group, the answer would be no. Surprisingly, although the networks vary greatly in the emphasis and resources devoted to quality control, catalogers expressed about equal measures of satisfaction or dissatisfaction with the records in their network whether they worked with RLIN, OCLC, or WLN. In general catalogers appeared to believe that all the data bases contained a high proportion of substandard records. Their attitudes confirm Luquire's findings—catalogers equate quality with past in-house practice and not with present network records. On the other hand, administrators appeared more concerned with computer downtime, hit rate, and costs than with the quality of the records available from their networks. In fact, two of the libraries, Berkeley and the University of Washington, had switched a large portion of their cataloging activities to OCLC because of that network's hit rate, despite the fact that library literature is filled with articles discussing the high number of duplicate records and errors in the OCLC data base.

But, of course, the sample libraries form only a miniscule fraction of all the network customers, and library literature does reveal instances of libraries joining RLG because of the presumption that high-quality records are guaranteed by the prestige of RLG's inputting libraries (Kallenbach and Jacobson, 1980; Dailey et al., 1982). That same literature also reveals professional awareness and approval of WLN's linked computer authority files and human revision process (Miles-Culp, 1979). Thus there is some evidence to support the contention that linkage of standards and costs affects networks in two ways:

1. Networks actively lobby for consideration of costs and rate of patron use during the standard-setting process.
2. Networks publicize their standard-setting enforcement activities in order to attract customers and increase revenues.

While catalogers and network personnel are not necessarily in conflict during the standard-setting process, and in fact usually interact fairly harmoniously, they do not define quality records or quality control in precisely the same way. Catalogers stress internal consistency and total coverage of every data element. Networks both broaden and narrow this vision. Their evaluation of standards discards total emphasis on internal consistency and substitutes a more balanced menu of consistency, costs, and customer use. For this very reason, there is also less emphasis on total coverage and more interest in developing compact records representing data of greatest interest to users.

Previous chapters have already included discussion of library administrators' perception of the strong need to contain costs related to automating library functions. Unlike networks, libraries are unable to recover expended funds through increased patron usage. Of course, it can be argued that over time this customer support and satisfaction is translated into increased public funding of libraries, but there is little evidence to support this view. Over the past decade, public support has eroded not only for academic libraries but for their chief users—students and faculty members. Therefore, although the direct patrons of academic libraries may be experiencing increased satisfaction because of newly automated services, the general public has shown strong resistance to increased funding for universities in particular, and public institutions in general. In California, where five of the six sample libraries are located, the combination of the tax-cutting initiative, Proposition 13, and the economic recession of the early 1980's severely affected public financing of higher education. And in Washington State, the acute effects of the economic recession also caused a squeeze on the budget of the University of Washington. Thus the early 1980's formed a period of intense financial pressures for the sample libraries without much prospect of bailout through increased patron support. Administrators' concerns about costs naturally affect their definition of what quality cataloging standards should contain. Then too, the period of reduced funding for libraries also coincides with the implementation of AACR2 and, as has been noted, most administrators interviewed did not feel that the revision of standards produced enough benefits to justify the increased costs to their libraries. But at least as important as cost considerations to administrators is what they are learning about their patrons. The sample libraries have either developed online catalogs or are in the process of planning the implementation of a computerized public access catalog. In addition, the library literature is filled with studies of patron reaction to this new cataloging format and service. All these studies reveal that patrons like the new format and prefer to search brief cataloging records. Although they are encountering difficulty executing subject searches, they are also learning to search for subject content using key words (distinctive words, especially in the title) instead of the carefully controlled vocabulary of the cataloger. Most important is the growing realization of administrators that standards developed to support the organization of 3 × 5 cards in the traditional catalog, even though they have been somewhat revised to accommodate a machine-readable format, may actually inhibit patrons from being able to exploit the new online format and produce the precise doses of information that they are seeking.

In the online environment, for instance, it has become technically feasible to input the table of contents of any item. Inclusion of such material would provide patrons with new ways to subject-search for library materials to locate very specialized information. Present cataloging codes, however, still focus almost exclusively on describing the major subjects of books or other library materials and make no provision for including indexes to specialized sections of those materials.

Ake I. Koel is one administrator who questions the value to the library and to the user of both the old cataloging and the new network quality control standards (Koel, 1981:220–222):

Given the impact of the cost of cataloging on library budgets, economic optimization of bibliographic control has to be very high on any library's agenda, especially in these times of financial instability and shrinking budgets. One of the roads open to us if we are to pursue economic optimization is to analyze the situation, starting with the user and then working our way back to the codes.

. . . Any large scale changes in the current MARC format would be expensive, to say nothing of the existing data bases and archive tapes that would have to be tampered with if such a change took place. This state of affairs heralds a growing rigidity of bibliographic control in the future brought upon not by cataloging codes but by automation software. There also seems to be a kind of Parkinson's Law lurking here: "any automation program tends to expand to satisfy all possible expectations," without regard to diminishing returns.

In her review of library research on the online catalog, Margaret Beckman also concludes that the user may be ill served by the rigidity of catalogers' codes and of corresponding network software built to accommodate those codes. Like other administrators, she is concerned both by the costs of standards and their benefits to users. In other words, even if costs could be reduced, there is growing concern among administrators and researchers that present standards act as potential barriers to full patron use of, or experimentation with, rapidly developing new technologies. Beckman, therefore, poses a series of questions (1982:2047):

Are the standards, the conventions, the philosophies developed for the card catalog environment appropriate today? Are standards, conventions and philosophies developed for the generation of mainframe, centralized computer facilities and networks economically sensible in the world of rapidly changing microprocessor and telecommunications technologies?

... Let us not repeat the mistakes of the 60's and 70's in which we used computers to produce, perhaps more efficiently, manual catalog products and access. Instead we must define user needs, not in terms of what we can and currently do provide, but in terms of what the new technology allows. In designing online catalogs for the 80's, while we must be mindful of our past experience, we must also remember to ask ourselves the following questions:

Has the user been better served by the introduction of AACR2, if it has meant increasing backlogs in the cataloging departments of many academic libraries?

Will the user be better served by a system so expensive that there will be insufficient money to provide either sufficient terminals or the desired response time?

Can we not find a compromise which allows us to harness the newest technologies to user needs—user needs which are identified independent of traditional systems, philosophies, and standards?

Thus some administrators appear to be moving toward a radical redefinition of cataloging standards and quality controls. Of course, not all, or even most, administrators have adopted an extreme position. No one interviewed at the sample libraries even suggested that cataloging standards might be dispensable or subject to constant change. In fact the contrary situation was prevalent. Most administrators were worried about the increasing rapidity of catalog code revisions and decried their costs to libraries.

Still, the Beckman article is not unique in its questioning of the rationale for present cataloging standards. Its stress on analysis of user needs and performance as the primary means of developing standards and defining quality is echoed in other articles by noted library administrators. In addition, library literature is beginning to include challenges to the sanctity of the cataloging codes and sometimes even to the future utility of networks.

One of the really significant results of the development of an online catalog is that administrators and researchers can unobtrusively watch and record patron searches for library materials without their observations affecting the behavior of the person using the catalog. They can also program terminals to display questions to patrons as they engage in information searches. Because activity at the terminal can be easily observed and all patron online search strategies can be recorded and diagnosed, a wealth of new material about patron information-seeking behavior is now available. Seeing how users operate at the catalog, instead of asking them to provide a later explanation of their behavior (one of the most popular methods for studying card catalog use) is profoundly affecting library administrators and forcing them to reevaluate long-standing library practices and values. In fact, interviews with some administrators at the six libraries showed that the heightened impact of visible user behavior occurs even when reported online results (e.g. Brownrigg and Lynch, 1983) simply verify previous research (e.g. Palmer, 1972) based on questionnaires and interviews. Thus administrators are becoming familiar with powerful evidence showing that most users are seeking only a few of the items on the bibliographic record and are receptive to using key words to search for subjects. Moreover, they are not seeking retrieval of all titles that the library holds on a specific subject—they simply want a manageable and useful list in their subject area (Brownrigg and Lynch, 1983:106). Almost every study reveals that online users seldom seek information or define quality cataloging in ways that correspond to cataloging theory or support the maintenance of present codes and standards. In fact, the visibility of online catalog use creates data that leads researchers to question not only the present utility of codes, but to ponder whether they ever satisfied user needs. Thus Larson and Graham note (1983:101):

The differences between searching patterns in the online catalog and the card catalog suggest (what many librarians have suspected) that subject searching in card catalogs is limited not because users don't want to do subject searches, but because the way subjects are presented and arranged in card catalogs is not conducive to use. As Mooer's law of information retrieval states, "An information retrieval system will tend not to be used when it is more painful and troublesome for a customer to have information than for him not to have it." When users have a better way to get at subjects, they will tend to do subject searches, and the online catalog certainly can provide a less "painful and troublesome" method.

And Edwin Brownrigg, one of the developers of the University of California's online catalog, also cites the visible results of user searches to challenge the implicit assumption that creators of catalogs in any format work from a defensible knowledge base when developing cataloging systems, standards, and controls (1983:105):

If the studies of patron access and other comments on online catalogs have any clear theme, it is that many of our assumptions about what type of access the user desires are without foundation. In a very real sense we have provided a modern, computerized version of a manual system that seems to have had some rather serious flaws. Automated systems allow the user to circumvent some of these problems but as much by unforeseen application of user ingenuity as by any great insight on the part of system designers.

Administrators appear to be moving toward a cataloging standard stressing flexibility, utility, and economy. They do so because available evidence appears to support the view that patrons primarily view the catalog as a finding, and not as a bibliographic device. Patrick Wilson, basing his analysis on cognitive authority of catalogers (or, more precisely, on their

lack of cognitive authority and subject expertise), also concludes that the catalog is best used as a finding tool (1983:16):

The upshot of all this is, as far as I'm concerned, that the unique
contribution of the catalog is, after all, just what most people have
always agreed it had to be, to help locate copies of books and texts
that may have been learned about elsewhere. It has to be a local
finding device. Its service as a convenient selective guide to the subject
contents of the collection is secondary to this. It is in many ways a
superficial bibliographical instrument, but this should cause no em-
barrassment; it is not meant to be, and should not try to be, the
complete and definitive guide to the bibliographical universe, but an
essential local supplement to the complex apparatus of means of discovery. In its revolutionary online form, that's what it will still be.
But if all goes well, it will be an excitingly flexible and comfortable
piece of bibliographical apparatus.

Since the data presented in Chapter 4 indicates that catalogers
are experiencing decreased opportunities to specialize in a subject area or review all the current literature in their subject
speciality, it seems reasonable to expect increased attacks by
administrators and/or researchers on catalogers' continued
ability to maintain and develop authoritative bibliographic files.

It does appear that the administrator/researcher standard of
utility, flexibility, and compactness has few links to the catalogers' codes that stress consistency, complexity, and completeness. In some ways it can be argued that the standards developed
by network personnel bridge the gap between the two groups,
embracing consistency and economy, utility and complexity.
Still, it is obvious that network systems derive their structure
from catalogers' codes, not from analysis of user behavior or
desires. Moreover, network emphasis on cost focuses on cost
recovery through increased patronage, not on cost saving, the
major strategy of library administrators. Thus catalogers, network personnel, administrators, and researchers differ greatly
in their definitions of cataloging quality and in emphasis on
developing and monitoring quality control activities. It does
not seem, however, that network development per se is the
major reason for these differing values. In fact, the brief analysis in this chapter shows that network development is gen-

erally supportive of cataloging standards. Visibility undermines cataloging standards although not primarily because
cataloging can be seen throughout the network system. It does
so because user behavior now also can be observed on the computer terminal, thereby creating new insights for administrators. Once this occurs, pressure grows for library administrators
to redefine quality control as response to patron needs rather
than adherence to cataloging codes and monitoring of catalogers' performance.

Whether in fact they will be successful against the idealism
and tenacity that catalogers devote to perpetuating their codes,
or against the organizational and technical expertise of network personnel, is still very much in question, and I personally
doubt that they will prevail. History, after all, records far more
victories for the zealot than the systems analyst or the cost
accountant. Moreover, despite the fact that cataloging standards and rules have been much maligned, the weight of evidence supports catalogers' assertions that it is their expertise,
their esoteric body of knowledge, that is responsible for patron
success in locating materials in both card and online catalogs.
Numerous studies have validated this conclusion. In fact, a
1979 review of all major card catalog use studies (Hafter, 1979),
revealed that users were extremely successful locating material in the card catalog. Patron frustration resulted not from
the catalog but from the face that a library either had not
purchased the desired item or that it was out in circulation. In
like manner, while the fixation of catalogers on their code and
on their peers seems to fly in the face of the prevailing "customer is always right" ideology of the library profession, it
squares perfectly with one of the most highly quoted and approved adages of modern day managers: "If it ain't broke, don't
fix it."

Finally, although libraries may be evolving into high tech
institutions characterized by rapid change, there is scarce evidence that librarians are willing to change their work practices,
standards, and procedures at a corresponding pace. Indeed it
is hard to believe that library professionals in general, even
those outraged by catalogers' disinterest in studies of patron
use, would ever seriously consider abandoning the very codes

that buttress their claims to esoteric knowledge and professional status. And networks also have a built-in stake in defending those complex codes for, after all, if the bibliographic record becomes straightforward and consists of few data elements, it might be possible for libraries to use microcomputer programs and not networks to create most of their cataloging.

Thus the continuing vigor and faith of catalogers in defense of their standards, and the ability of cataloging masters to adapt to and ally themselves with technologically advanced organizations like networks, presages a future where catalogers will still retain a high degree of quality and social control over standard setting, monitoring, and enforcement within their profession.

CHAPTER VII

Summary and Conclusions

This case study was initiated to examine the impact of networks on the organization and quality of work of professional catalogers. Research centered on the role of standard setting and enforcement in an online environment. Such an environment is characterized not only by dependence on regional, national, and international computerized networks linking libraries, but also by rapid changes in technology and by the heightened visibility of work. In an online setting, visibility makes it possible to evaluate and monitor work, and also to determine whether libraries and library patrons reap full benefits from the information described and organized on bibliographic records using cataloging codes.

In general, interviews and the literature reviewed confirm the original hypothesis that increased reliance on networks creates a trend toward the deprofessionalization of cataloging. Control over the organization and scheduling of work is shown to be shifting from cataloging departments to library administrators and to network personnel. Moreover, the actual practice of cataloging is being restructured so that routine and standardized records available in the data base can be manipulated by library assistants and clerks, rather than catalogers. Administrators are decreeing that less time and effort be devoted to creating complex bibliographic records and/or local embellishments of a cataloging record. The material remaining to be organized by catalogers in many instances lacks significance, interest, and/or great scholarly value. Thus it appears clear that many aspects of network participation by libraries threaten the status, authority, and autonomy of professional catalogers and leads to deprofessionalization of their work.

The interviews and literature also reveal that networks depend on the work of catalogers, generally believe in and benefit from the codes they develop, and support the standard-setting activities of master catalogers and cataloging advisory groups. However, network personnel do part company with the majority of catalogers on the issue of the compactness of the bibliographic record. Network workers are interested in developing standardized formats that include all the elements required to access information about a specific library acquisition. They are not as concerned as catalogers about using the record to describe all bibliographic information about an item (e.g. detailed notes about its contents or added entries to identify some aspect of the item that is of local interest).

In order to promote conformity with network standards, these online institutions develop a variety of strategies. The most significant of the techniques used to foster adherence to network practices is the promotion of the error tally, a procedure based upon searching the data base, identifying substandard cataloging, and assigning errors to catalogers and cataloging departments. Other methods used by the networks include the development of buddy systems linking master and trainee cataloging departments, the bestowing of awards for quality network cataloging, and the co-opting of cataloger leaders through participation in significant advisory committees or through network delegation of revising powers to master catalogers (e.g. Project Enhance).

Network personnel are also shown to be responsive to issues of cost and are sometimes willing to relax their own standards when customers (i.e. library administrators) lobby for development of cheaper cataloging records. In particular, the positive response of all three networks (OCLC, RLIN, WLN) to the idea of expanding the types of material that could receive minimal cataloging, is a good example of the networks' cost consciousness and their resulting flexibility on the issue of developing and adhering to quality standards.

Conversely, this very flexibility and desire to mediate between cataloging and administrative visions of a bibliographic standard, makes it difficult to support the contention that networks are becoming agents both of quality control and social control of catalogers. Although network activities include all the elements for social control of work (the formulation and dissemination of standards of performance, the surveillance of performance, the sanctioning or reinforcement of desired behavior, the discovery and punishment of deviance), the collegial structure of the network tends to mitigate the impact of the controls placed upon catalogers and, in many instances, restores lost authority to them. It is true that network standards differ somewhat from cataloger standards, but unlike administrators, network personnel unite with catalogers in their faith in, and adherence to, a prevailing standard, defining quality work as conformity to cataloging codes. Since those codes are primarily the creation of master catalogers, network quality control enforcement contains a large component of self-monitoring of cataloging by accepted leaders of the profession.

Of course, the close cooperation between networks and catalogers, especially cataloging advisory groups, does not mean that their interests are identical or that their activities never produce negative consequences for each other. It does mean, however, that networks show signs of developing into professional organizations—institutions characterized by their ability to organize varied groups of professionals into collegial units that retain a high degree of autonomy and self-policing functions. And professional organizations often provide a framework for mediating between power blocs (e.g. cataloging peer groups and administrators) and linking them together through committee structures and personal contacts.

Thus the network connection appears to produce the threat of deprofessionalization for the vast majority of catalogers, combined with support of, and alliance to, the minority of cataloging masters and peer groups working with the networks. The rise of these peer groups and the identification of master catalogers are linked to the phenomenon of cataloging work made nationally visible through the network data base. Although this visibility can, and has, endangered the reputation of catalogers and cataloging departments, its more significant result has been the identification of network-defined, approved, and supported master catalogers. These catalogers become the present and future creators of cataloging codes and of many network input procedures. The networks also provide the framework for bringing catalogers together in advisory committees, thereby strengthening their links to their peers and to their host networks. Thus cataloging peer groups are growing in authority, power, and visibility at the same time that cataloging departments are shrinking in size, status, and significance within the overall structure of their libraries. As a result, network participation has led to a shift in catalogers' interest and support from in-house cataloging departments to network-initiated peer groups.

What appears to be developing as the result of the introduction of online network technology is some redefinition of cataloging leadership (cataloging departments versus peer groups), standards (elaborate versus standardized records), and quality control activities (human revision in the in-house cataloging department versus nationwide discovery of errors through the visibility of the computer terminal). In general, catalogers have accepted the need to adapt their codes to computer formats but have been unwilling to compromise their professional mandate to retain complete and complex description and linkage of materials and their subject contents. And in general, networks have approved of the cataloging codes, but have some reservations about the amount of description that should characterize the standardized catalog record.

If, in some sense, the growth of the network is a threat to the rigid traditional ideals and standards of the cataloger, it is because networks accept the concept that costs and customer requirements have an impact upon these codes. Administrators, however, have developed much more direct and vigorous attacks upon the sanctity of the cataloging codes. In many instances they are beginning to suggest that customer needs and costs incurred might be more important than code consistency or completeness. Although as yet only a few library administrators have used the library literature to direct attacks on catalogers' work, standards, and codes, these writers rank as leaders of the library profession whose views carry great influence. Moreover, the administrative attack is not based primarily on changes wrought by the network, but on the rapid pace of change that has now become the standard for the high technology environment of libraries. Another factor that has greatly undermined the faith of administrators in catalogers and their codes is the heightened visibility of patron search strategies at the online catalog. Once again it is not the network but the technology associated with computers that leads administrators to question whether codes were, are, or will be of great enough benefit to justify the costs incurred by libraries in adhering to them and by patrons in time spent trying to glean information from the intricacies of the bibliographic record.

Indeed, recent library literature provides evidence of the growing doubts of many professionals about the validity of traditional cataloging standards in the new online environment. As they examine the flexible and adaptive search strategies of patrons at the online catalog and find more and more evidence to support the belief that users desire a catalog that is a compact finding tool, they begin to question all the cataloging verities, including continued dependence on networks. Their thoughts turn to microcomputers and local programs that may automatically generate the simple records that patrons seem to want.

Conclusion

Central to the cataloging ethos is the fixation on consistency, complexity, quality standards, and quality controls based on the interpretation of acknowledged master catalogers. Linked to these factors are the catalogers' strong interests in their peers and their professional standards, and their apparent lack of concern about the library patron. Finally, the cataloger's work and vocabulary are imbued with a sense of moral righteousness that reflects the dedication of this professional to the search for ideal standards. The image that leaps to mind from this combination of factors is the Talmudic scholar—the seeker of truth for its own sake, the last of the just.

Fertile areas for research would involve case studies of the methods used by libraries to incorporate these inner directed workers into an organizational structure characterized by its extreme emphasis on serving and pleasing patrons. In fact, several studies have shown that reference librarians are so patron-oriented that they will attempt to satisfy all information requests even when their resources are out of date or inadequate. Two notable studies by Crowley and Childers (1971) and Peat, Marwick, and Mitchell (1975) indicate that the need to please customers is so overriding that reference librarians will provide some answer to patron queries even when they have inadequate information to base an answer upon. The result was that the patrons had barely one chance in two of receiving a correct factual response to a query posed to a reference librarian. Thus quality work to the reference librarian is sometimes evaluated not by the standard of work delivered but primarily by the level of satisfaction expressed by the customer.

Obviously a profession that can house such extreme types—talmudic scholars and patron groupies—and can still function in a high technology environment might provide some interesting models for other heterogeneous work groups. In particular, one wants to know what traits, if any, reference librarians and catalogers share in common and, if they can be discovered, are they the distinguishing characteristics of all library professionals?

Another area of research centers on the possible deprofessionalization of non-cataloging librarians. To date, many public service librarians believe that computer technology has elevated their status and anointed them as true professionals of the Information Age. They point to activities such as online reference searching and development of integrated information systems as examples of the expanded knowledge base they have developed. Increased status for systems and reference librarians does appear to be occurring. Still, it should be noted that the kind of work described may be capable of being restructured into smaller and simpler components and automated. Moreover, visibility of reference librarians' search strategies in the online reference data bases may, over time, erode their claims to specialized knowledge of subject areas or to generalized overviews of all relevant reference sources. Mistakes in search strategy are now recorded in the printout of the online reference search that is handed to the patron. The patron has an added incentive to evaluate this work because almost all libraries require users to pay for the costs of computer time utilized during the search. Therefore, if the online reference search is inadequate the user will have evidence of poor reference performance plus a relatively expensive bill to pay for the substandard work produced. These combined results could obviously have a negative impact on reference librarians' prestige within the academic community. Thus the same trends and technology that now threaten many catalogers' claims to professional status may soon afflict reference librarians.

One thing is certain: library dependence upon computers in general, and online networks in particular, forces reevaluation not only of traditional professional activities but of the standards upon which these activities are based. To date catalogers are the group of library professionals who have experienced the most direct consequences from the assault on standards and the threat to status that accompanies any proposed shifts in work. In general the group has suffered both a loss in numbers of jobs and in status within individual libraries. But catalogers, fueled by belief in the long-run utility of their standards, have been able to mount a counterattack and even wrest enhanced authority and status (albeit only for a small percentage of all catalogers) within the shelter of the developing network organization. They have strengthened their self-help groups and formed new and powerful alliances within the networks. Their ability to respond in this dynamic manner to a rapidly changing work environment appears to be fueled by their overwhelming commitment to, and belief in, their own quality standards. Their long-run success or failure will provide valuable guidelines for information workers as a whole about the utility of basing claims to professional status on quality control standards and code setting activities.

APPENDIX   A

Quality Control Questionnaire for Catalogers

1. What is "quality control"?
2. Where does the primary authority and responsibility for quality control lie?
3. What are the key issues of quality control at:
   a) the institutional level
   b) the local level
   c) the regional level
   d) the national/international level
4. Are bibliographic networks creating new national standards for cataloging quality?
5. What is the best way to promote cataloging information exchange at:
   a) the national level
   b) the regional level
   c) the local level
6. Is there a need for a periodic national forum for cataloging quality control?
7. What type of quality control activities are appropriate at each level of responsibility?
   a) individual cataloger
   b) individual library
   c) regional office
   d) network office
8. What do you think are your network's expectations regarding individual library quality control? Are they realistic?
9. Does your network provide error tallies? If so, what are their advantages or disadvantages?

10. How does your library make use of error tallies?
11. Are you familiar with any library peer groups? What are their major activities? How important are these activities?
12. What are the major quality control activities of your individual library?
13. Do you think that participation in online bibliographic networks leads to more or less cataloging quality? Why?
14. What effect has participation in online bibliographic networks had on:
    a) the status of catalogers
    b) the status of cataloging departments
    c) the status of library administrators
15. How long have you worked as a cataloger? How long in your present job?
16. Do you possess a library degree? What degree is it? When did you graduate?
17. Into which age category do you fall:
    a) 20–30
    b) 31–40
    c) 41–50
    d) 51–60
    e) Over 60
18. Sex of interviewee: Male–Female

APPENDIX B

Quality Control Questionnaire for Administrators

1. What are the procedures for evaluating the work of probationary employees in your cataloging department?
2. How long ago was the last original cataloger hired?
3. How long ago was the last professional cataloger hired?
4. Does your cataloging department revise the work of nonprobationary employees? If so, what is the process for providing feedback to:
   a) copy catalogers
   b) original catalogers
5. When working with (OCLC, RLIN, WLN) what requirements do you have for accepting copy found in the data base?
6. What percentage of your department's total cataloging comes from cataloging copy located in the network data base?
7. Your network provides monthly reports on the error rate for your library. Do you make use of these reports in any way? If so, how?
8. Has participation in an online network had any effect on your library's quality control procedures or standards? Please be specific.
9. Has the examination of cataloging copy located in the network data base affected your own library's cataloging practices? If so, how?
10. Does your library accept all contributed copy?
11. Is there a preferred institutions list? If so, how are the institutions selected?
12. What is the yearly volume of original cataloging at your library?
13. How is the output of original catalogers measured? What is measured? Are there minimum production standards?

14. Is there a backlog? If so, how large is it? How old are the oldest items in it?
15. How has the implementation of AACR2 affected your cataloging department? What impact has it had on the library as a whole?
16. Does your cataloging department do minimal level cataloging? What kind of material is cataloged in this way?
17. Do you think that cataloging, as a professional activity, has developed more or less status as the result of your library's participation in an online network? Why?
18. How many original catalogers are employed at your library?
19. How many copy catalogers are employed at your library?
20. How many items were cataloged in 1982/83?
21. Does your library have, or is it planning to develop, an online catalog? If so, what is the composition of the membership of the online catalog planning group?

APPENDIX C

Computer Fields and Subfields

A *field* contains information that forms a logical unit. A *record* is the collection of fields containing information about a separately cataloged item. Each record has one fixed field and a number of variable fields.

Fixed Field

Each record contains one field that carries information in coded form. This field is known as the *fixed field* because the size of the field does not vary. In general, fixed field information describes the work cataloged and the record itself, and is usually information that does not appear on a typical printed catalog record. Inclusion of coded information in the fixed field allows networks to take advantage of the computer's capabilities for data manipulation and retrieval.

Variable Fields

Fields that contain information such as main entry, title or a note are known as *variable fields* because the fields vary in length, depending on the work being described. Each variable field is identified by a three-digit code called a *tag*.

Subfields

Within each field, information is divided into smaller logical units. Each smaller unit is called a *subfield*. For example, a typical imprint contains three subfields: place, publisher, and date.

Bibliography

Alex, N. (1969) *Black in Blue: A Study of the Negro Policeman.* New York, Appleton-Century Crofts.

Allison, Anne Marie and Ann Allan (1979) *OCLC: A National Library Network.* Short Hills, N.J., Enslow Publishers.

Asher, Richard E. (1980) "Anglo-American Cataloging Rules II and Card Catalog Maintenance." *Catholic Library World* 52(Dec.):226–228.

Association of Research Libraries (1976) *The Library of Congress as the National Bibliographic Center.* Washington, D.C. Association of Research Libraries.

Atkinson, Hugh (1979) "The Electronic Catalog." In *The Nature and Future of the Catalog: Proceedings of the ALA's Information Science and Automation Division's 1975 and 1977 Institutes.* Edited by Maurice J. Freedman. Phoenix, Ariz., Oryx Press.

Avram, Henriette D. et al. (1983) "Status of Processing Services Automation in the Library of Congress." *Information Technology and Libraries* 2(June):135–141.

Baldwin, Paul Evered (1976) "Bibliographic Control Problems and Organizational Change Issues Posed by the Implementation of a Computer Based Co-Operative Cataloging System." Unpublished M.B.A. Thesis. Simon Fraser University.

Ball, Donald W. (1974) "Replacement Processes in Work Organizations: Task Evaluation and the Case of Professional Football." *Sociology of Work and Occupations* 1(May):197–219.

Beckman, Margaret M. (1982) "Online Catalogs and Library Users." *Library Journal* 107(Nov. 15):2043–2047.

Bell, Daniel (1973) *The Coming of Post Industrial Society.* New York, Basic Books.

Berelson, Bernard, ed. (1949) *Education for Librarianship*. Chicago, University of Chicago Graduate Library School.

Birdsall, William F. (1982) "Librarianship, Professionalism, & Social Change." *Library Journal* 107(Feb. 1):223–226.

Bishop, David F. (1983) "The CLR OPAC Study Analysis of ARL User Responses." *Information Technology and Libraries* 2(Sept.):315–321.

Blakenship, Ralph L. (1980) *Colleagues in Organizations*. Huntington, N.Y., Krieger Publishing Co.

Blishen, B. R. (1969) *Doctors and Doctrines: The Ideology of Medical Care in Canada*. Toronto, University of Toronto Press.

Boissonas, Christian M. (1979) "The Quality of the OCLC Bibliographic Records: The Cornell University Law Library Experience." *Law Library Journal* 72(Winter):80–85.

Borricaud, Francois (1979) "Individualistic Mobilization and the Crisis of Professional Authority." *Daedalus* 18(Spring):12–18.

Braden, Sally, John D. Hall and Helen H. Britten (1980) "Utilization of Personnel and Bibliographic Resources for Cataloging by OCLC Participating Libraries." *Library Resources and Technical Services* 24 (Spring): 135–154.

Brown, Georgia (1981) "AACR2: OCLC's Implementation and Data Base Conversion." *Journal of Library Automation* 14(Sept.):161–173.

Brown, Roland (1982) "Network Level Decisions." In *Information Technology: Critical Choices for Library Decision Makers*. Pittsburgh, Dekker, pp. 178–189.

Brownrigg, Edwin B. and Clifford A. Lynch (1983) "Online Catalogs: Through a Glass Darkly." *Information Technology and Libraries* 2(Mar.):104–115.

Bucher, Rue and Joan Stelling (1980) "Four Characteristics of Professional Organizations." In Ralph L. Blakenship, ed. *Colleagues in Organizations*. Huntington, N.Y., Krieger, pp. 121–144.

Burger, Robert H. (1983) "Data Definition & the Decline of Cataloging Quality." *Library Journal* 108(Oct. 15):1924–1926.

Caplow, Theodore and Reece J. McGee (1958) *The Academic Marketplace*. New York, Basic Books.

Cargille, Douglas A. (1982) "Variant Edition Cataloging on OCLC: Input or Adapt?" *Library Resources and Technical Services* 26(Jan.–Mar.):47–51.

"The Catalogerless Society" (1983). *American Libraries* 14(Dec.):730.

Chaplin, A. H. (1975) "Basic Bibliographic Control: Plans for a World System." *Aslib Proceedings* 27(Feb.):48–56.

Chapple, Sharon (1974) *Canadian Experience with MARC*. Ottawa, National Library of Canada.

Chwe, Steven Seokho (1976) "A Comparative Study of Librarians' Job
    Satisfaction: Catalogers and Reference Librarians in Univer-
    sity Libraries." Unpublished Ph. D. dissertation. University of
    Pittsburgh Graduate Library School.

Coser, Rose Laub (1961) "Insulation From Observability and Types
    of Social Conformity." *American Sociological Review* 26(Fall):
    28–39.

Crawford, Walt (1983) "Long Searches, Slow Response: Recent Ex-
    perience on RLIN." *Information Technology and Libraries*
    2(June):176–182.

Crowley, Terence and T. A. Childers (1971) *Information Service in
    Public Libraries: Two Studies.* Metuchen, N.J., Scarecrow Press.

Cutter, Charles A. (1904) *Rules for a Dictionary Catalog.* 4th ed. Wash-
    ington, D.C., U.S. Government Printing Office.

Dailey, K. M. et al. (1982) "RLIN and OCLC Side by Side: Two Com-
    parison Studies." In *Agencies in Library Administration and
    Organization.* vol. 1. Greenwich, Conn., JAI Press, pp. 69–125.

Das Gupta, K. (1981) "Impact of Technology on the Role of the Tech-
    nical Services Librarian of Academia in the USA." *International
    Library Review* 13(Oct.):397–408.

De Gennaro, Richard (1981) "Libraries and Networks in Transition:
    Problems and Prospects for the 1980's." *Library Journal* 106(May
    15):1045–1049.

Denzin, Norman K. (1968) "Incomplete Professionalization: The Case
    of Pharmacy." *Social Forces* 46(Mar.):375–381.

Dowell, Arlene Taylor (1976) *Cataloging With Copy: A Decisionmak-
    er's Handbook.* Littleton, Colo., Libraries Unlimited.

Drake, Miriam (1977) "The Management of Libraries as Professional
    Organizations." *Special Libraries* 68(May/June):181–186.

Draper, Hal (1964) "Librarian vs. Scholar-User." *Library Journal*
    89(May 1):1907–1910.

Drucker, Peter (1969) *The Age of Discontinuity.* New York, Harper.

Druschel, Jocelyn (1981) "Cost Analysis of an Automated and Manual
    Cataloging and Book Processing System." *Journal of Library
    Automation* 14(Mar.):24–49.

Etzioni, Amitai and R. Remp (1973) *Technological Shortcuts to Social
    Change.* New York, Russell Sage.

Etzioni, Amitai, ed. (1969) *The Semi-Professions and Their Organi-
    zation.* New York, Free Press.

Evans, Glyn T. (1978) "Constituency Concerns in OCLC Management:
    User, Library, Network, OCLC." In *Requiem for the Card Cat-
    alog: Management Issues in Automated Cataloging.* Ed. by Dan-
    iel Gore, Joseph Kimbrough and Peter Spyers-Duran. Westport,
    Conn., Greenwood Press, pp. 40–55.

Freedman, Maurice J. (1984) "Must We Limit the Catalog?" *Library Journal* 109(Feb. 15):322–324.

Freidson, Eliot (1970) *Profession of Medicine: A Study of the Sociology of Applied Knowledge.* New York, Dodd Mead.

Friedman, L. M. (1965) "Freedom of Contract and Occupational Licensing 1890–1910: A Legal and Social Study." *California Law Review* 53(May):487–534.

Gershuny, Jonathan D. (1977) "Post Industrial Society: The Myth of the Service Economy." *Futures* (April):103–114.

Gilb, C. L. (1966) *Hidden Hierarchies: The Professions and the Government.* New York, Harper and Row.

Glaser, Barney (1964) *Organizational Scientists: Their Professional Careers.* New York, Irvington.

Glazer, Nathan (1978) "The Attack on the Professions." *Commentary* 66(Nov.):34–40.

Goode, W. J. (1961) "The Librarian: From Occupation to Profession?" *Library Quarterly* 31(Oct.):306–321.

Gore, Daniel (1964) "Subject Cataloging: Some Consideration of Costs." *Library Journal* 89 (Oct. 1):3699–3703.

Gorman, Michael (1979) "Doing Away With Technical Services Departments." *American Libraries* 10(July/Aug.):435–437.

———. (1978) "The Anglo-American Cataloging Rules: Second Edition." *Library Resources and Technical Services* 22:209–213.

Greenwood, E. (1957) "Attributes of a Profession." *Social Work* 2(July):45–55.

Hafter, Ruth (1979) "The Performance of Card Catalogs: A Review of the Research." *Library Research: An International Journal* 1(Nov.):33–64.

Hagler, Ronald and Peter Simmons (1982) *The Bibliographic Record and Information Technology.* Chicago, American Library Association.

Hall, R. H. (1968) "Professionalization and Bureaucratization." *American Sociology Review* 33(Feb.):92–105.

Hapgood, David (1974) *The Screwing of the Average Man.* Garden City, N.J., Doubleday.

Haug, Marie (1975) "The Deprofessionalization of Everyone?" *Sociological Focus* 6(Aug.):197–213.

Hewitt, Joe A. (1976) "The Impact of OCLC." *American Libraries* 7(May):268–275.

———. (1976a) "The Impact of On-Line Cataloging on the Operation of Academic Libraries: A Study of the Charter Members of the Ohio College Library Center." Unpublished Ph.D. dissertation. University of California.

Holley, Edward G. (1984) "The Merwine Case and the MLS: Where Was ALA?" *American Libraries* 15(May):327–330.

Holley, R. P. (1981) "Futures of Catalogers and Cataloging." *Journal of Academic Librarianship* 7(May):90–93.

Hudson, Judith (1981) "Revisions to Contributed Cataloging in a Cooperative Data Base." *Journal of Library Automation* 14(June):116–120.

Hughes, Everett C. (1958) *Men and Their Work.* Glencoe, Ill., Free Press.

Information Technology: Critical Choices for Library Decision Makers. (1982) Ed. by A. Kent and I. J. Galvin. Pittsburgh, Dekker.

International Federation of Library Associations (1974) *International Standard Bibliographic Description for Monographic Publications.* London.

Intner, Sheila S. (1985) "A Giant Step Backward for Technical Services." *Library Journal* 110(Apr. 15):43–45.

Jacob, Mary Ellen, Richard Woods and Mary Yarborough (1979) *On-Line Resource Sharing 11: A Comparison of OCLC Incorporated, Research Libraries Information Network, and Washington Library Network.* San Jose, Calif., CLASS.

Jamous, H. and B. Peloille (1970) "Changes in the French University-Hospital System." In J. A. Jackson, ed. *Professions and Professionalization.* Cambridge, Eng., Cambridge University Press.

Jones, Robert E. (1982) "The Recent Transformation of WLN Governance." *Resource Sharing and Library Networks* 1(Winter/ Spring):67–84.

Kallenbach, Susan and Susan Jacobson (1980) "Staff Response to Changing Systems: From Manual to OCLC to RLIN." *Journal of Academic Librarianship* 6(May):264–267.

Kaske, Neal T. et al. (1983) "A Comparative Study of Online Public Access Catalogs: An Overview and Application of Findings." Dublin, Ohio, OCLC.

Katz, Fred E. (1970) *Autonomy and Organization: The Limits of Social Control.* New York, Random House.

Kayner, Nedra L. (1978) *Unit Time Cost Study of the Cataloging Unit Technical Services Division, Tucson Public Library.* Tucson Public Library, Ariz.

Kelm, Carol R. (1978) "The Historical Development of the Second Edition of the Anglo-American Cataloging Rules." *Library Resources and Technical Services* 22(Jan.):22–28.

Kemp, Elaine et al. (1981) "A Comparison of OCLC, RLG/RLIN, and WLN." *Journal of Library Automation* 14(Sept.):215–230.

Kennedy, Gail (1980) "Technical Processing Librarians in the 1980's:

Current Trends and Future Forecasts." University of Kentucky Libraries. *Occasional Papers* 1(Aug.):1–13.

Kilgour, Frederick G. (1983) "Public Policy and National and International Networks." *Information Technology and Libraries* 2(Sept.):239–245.

Kochen, Manfred and A. Bertrand Segur (1970) "Effects of Cataloging Volume at the Library of Congress on the Total Cataloging Costs of American Research Libraries." American Society for Information Science. *Journal.* (Mar./Apr.):112–127.

Koel, Ake I. (1981) "Bibliographic Control at the Crossroads: Do We Get Our Money's Worth?" *Journal of Academic Librarianship* 6(Apr.):220–222.

Krieger, Tillie, ed. (1976) "Catalogs and Catalogers: Evolution Through Revolution." *Journal of Academic Librarianship* 2(Apr.):173–180.

Larson, Magali S. (1977) *The Rise of Professionalism.* Berkeley, University of California Press.

Larson, Ray R. and Vicki Graham (1983) "Monitoring and Evaluating MELVYL." *Information Technology and Libraries* 2(Mar.):93–104.

Light, Donald W. (1971) "Psychiatry and Suicide: The Management of a Mistake." *Journal of Sociology* 77(July):821–837.

Lopata, Helene Z. (1976) "Expertization of Everyone and the Revolt of the Client." *Sociological Quarterly* (Autumn):435–437.

Luquire, William (1983) "Attitudes Toward Automation/Innovation in Academic Libraries." *Journal of Academic Librarianship* 8(Jan.):344–351.

———. (1976) "Selected Factors Affecting Library Staff Perceptions of an Innovative System: A Study of ARL Libraries in OCLC." Unpublished Ph.D. dissertation. Indiana University Graduate Library School.

MARC Formats for Bibliographic Data (1980–). Washington, D.C., Automated Systems Office. Library of Congress.

Markuson, Barbara Evans (1976) "The Ohio College Library Center: A Study of Factors Affecting the Adaption of Libraries to Online Networks." *Library Technology Reports* 12.

Martell, Charles (1981) "The War of AACR2: Victors or Victims?" *Journal of Academic Librarianship* 7(Mar.):4–8.

Martin, Murray S. (1981) *Issues in Personnel Management in Academic Libraries.* Greenwich, Conn., JAI Press.

Martin, Susan K. (1982) "Governance Issues for Automated Library Networks: The Impact of, and Implications for, Large Research Libraries." Unpublished Ph.D. dissertation. University of California, Berkeley, School of Library and Information Studies.

————. (1981) *Library Networks, 1981–82*. White Plains, N.Y., Knowledge Industry Publications.

————. (1979) "Upgrading 'Brief' and 'Dirty' Data." *American Libraries* 10(Apr.):210–222.

Maxwell, Margaret F. (1980) *Handbook for AACR2*. 2nd ed. Chicago, American Library Association.

McPherson, Dorothy et al. (1982) "Building a Merged Bibliographic Database: The University of California Experience." *Information Technology and Libraries* 1(Dec.):370–380.

Meyer, Richard W. (1980) "Library Professionalism and the Democratic Way." *Journal of Academic Librarianship* 6(Nov.):277–281.

Miles-Culp, Gwen (1979) "Authority Control Within the Washington Library Network Computer System." In *Authority Control: The Key to Tomorrow's Catalog. Proceedings of the 1979 Library and Information Technology Association Institutes.* Ed. by Mary W. Ghikas. Phoenix. Ariz., Oryx Press, pp. 62–84.

Montagna, P. D. (1968) "Professionalization and Bureaucratization in Large Professional Organizations." *American Journal of Sociology* 74(Sept.):138–145.

Morita, Ichiko (1983) "Quality Control of Copy Cataloging in an Online Environment." *Research Libraries in OCLC: A Quarterly* 11(July):1–3.

Mulkay, M. J. and A. T. Williams (1971) "A Sociological Study of the Physics Department." *British Journal of Sociology* 22(Mar.):68–82.

Nasatir, Marilyn (1983) "Machine Readable Data Base Files and Networks." *Information Technology and Libraries* 2(June):159–164.

National Library of Canada (1974) *Canadian National Bibliographic Data Base Study Report*. Ottawa.

North, J. (1977) "Librarianship: A Profession?" *Canadian Library Journal* 34(Aug.):253–257.

OCLC, Inc. (1980) "Questions and Answers." Columbus, Ohio, OCLC.

OCLC Newsletter, 1967–1983. Columbus, Ohio.

OCLC Online Computer Library Center. *Annual Reports* 1972/73–1983/84.

————. (Nov. 28, 1983) "Newsrelease—California State College San Bernadino Inputs Ten Millionth Record into OCLC Database."

OCLC. Pricing Committee (1983). "OCLC FY 1984–FY 1988 Pricing Strategy Recommendation Review." Dublin, Ohio.

OCLC. Users Council. "Minutes." 1977–1984.

OCLC Seeks Copyright Protection for Its Data Base" (1983). *Library Journal* 108(Feb.1):161–162.

OCLC Users Council Eyes Governance, Visibility." (1981). *Library Journal* 106(May):926–927.

Ohio College Library Center (1977) "OCLC Level I and Level K Input Standards." *OCLC Technical Bulletin* Number 30. Columbus, Ohio.

———. (1972) "Standards for Input Cataloging." Columbus, Ohio.

Oglebay Institute on Quality Control (1983) *Proceedings.* November 12–14, 1982. Pittsburgh Regional Library Center; OCLC On-Line Computer Library Center.

Overton, C. M. and Allan Seal (1979) *Cataloging Costs in the UK.* Bath University Library.

Palmer, Richard M. (1972) *Computerizing the Card Catalog in the University Library: A Survey of User Requirements.* Littleton, Colo., Libraries Unlimited.

Pavalko, Ronald M. (1971) *Sociology of Occupations and Professions.* Itaska, Ill., Peacock Publishers.

Peat, Marwick and Mitchell Company (1975) *California Public Library Systems: A Comprehensive Review With Guidelines for the Next Decade.* Los Angeles.

Perrucci, R. and J. E. Gerstl (1969) *Profession without Community: Engineers in American Society.* New York, Random House.

Pince, C. (1976) "Question of Motive." Cornell University Library. *Bulletin* 201(July):14–15.

Preston, G. A. (1982) "Foot in Both Camps: Using RLIN and OLCL." *Library Journal* 107(Oct. 15):1948–1949.

Reader, W. J. (1966) *Professional Men—The Rise of the Professional Classes in Nineteenth Century England.* London, Weidenfeld and Nicholson.

Reeves, William Joseph (1980) *Librarians as Professionals: The Occupation's Impact on Library Work Arrangements.* Lexington, Mass., D.C. Health.

Reisman, David (1964) *Constraint and Variety in American Education.* New York, Random House.

Reisman, L. and J. H. Rohrer (1957) *Change and Dilemma in the Nursing Profession.* New York, Charles Putnam's Sons.

Research Libraries Group (1981) "RLG Document Identification: RLG Bibliographic Standards." Stanford, Calif.

Roth, Julius A. (1974) "Professionalism, the Sociologist's Decoy." *Sociology of Work and Occupations* 1(Feb.):6–23.

Roughton, Michael (1980) "OCLC Serials Records: Errors, Omissions and Dependability." *Journal of Academic Librarianship* 5:316–320.

Ryan, Mary J. (1967) "Librarians' Perceptions of Librarianship." Unpublished Ph.D. dissertation. University of Southern California.

Scherba, Beverly (1974) "Terminal Illness for the Professional Cataloger." American Library Association. *Bulletin* 44(July):30–31.

Schoenung, James Gerald (1981) "The Quality of the Member Input Monograph Records in the OCLC On-line Union Catalog." Unpublished Ph.D. dissertation. Drexel University.

Scott, W. Richard (1964) "Reactions to Supervision in a Heteronomous Professional Organization." *Administrative Science Quarterly* 10:65–81.

Seal, Allan (1983) "Experiments With Full and Short Entry Catalogues: A Study of Library Needs." *Library Resources and Technical Services* 27(Apr./June):144–155.

Shaffer, D. E. (1968) *The Maturity of Librarianship as a Profession.* Metuchen, N.J., Scarecrow Press.

Simonds, Michael J. (1984) "Database Limitations and Online Catalogs." *Library Journal* 109(Feb. 15):329–330.

Sonoma State University (1983) "Student Telephone Survey and Ranking of Campus Services." Rohnert Park, Calif.

Soules, A. (1983) "Deterioration of Quality Cataloging." *Library Journal* 108(Jan. 1):27–29.

Spyers-Duran, Peter (1978) "The Effects of Automation on Organizational Change, Staffing, and Human Relations in Catalog Departments." In *Requiem for the Card Catalog: Management Issues in Automated Cataloging.* Ed. by Daniel Gore, Joseph Kimbrough and Peter Spyers-Duran. Westport, Conn., Greenwood Press, pp. 29–39.

Starr, Paul (1983) *The Social Transformation of Medicine.* New York, Basic Books.

Stelling, Joan and Rue Bucher (1972) "Autonomy and Monitoring on Hospital Wards." *Sociological Quarterly* 13(Fall):431–446.

Swank, Raynard Coe (1944) "Subject Catalogs, Classifications, or Bibliographies? A Review of Critical Discussions, 1876–1942." *Library Quarterly* 14(Oct.):316–332.

Tolle, John E. et al. (1983) "Current Utilization of Online Catalogs: Transaction Log Analysis." Dublin, Ohio, OCLC.

Toohey, Barbara and Joan Biermann (1964) "The Age of the Mass-Produced Gargoyle." *Library Journal* 89(Oct.1):3698–3699.

Toren, Nina (1975) "Deprofessionalization and its Sources: A Preliminary Analysis." *Sociology of Work and Occupations* 2(Nov.):323–337.

United States Department of Labor, Employment and Training Administration (1977) *Dictionary of Occupational Titles.* 4th Ed. Washington, D.C., U.S. Government Printing Office.

United States National Commission on Library and Information Science (1975) *Toward a National Program for Library and Information Services: Goals for Action.* Washington, D.C., U.S. Government Printing Office.

Van Houten, Stephen (1981) "In the Iron Age of Cataloging." *Library Resources and Technical Services* 25(Oct.-Dec.):362–373.

Veaner, Allen B. (1985) "1985 to 1995: The Next Decade in Librarianship, Part 1." *College and Research Libraries* 46(May):209–229.

Verona, Eva (1959) "Literary Unit Versus Bibliographic Unit." *Libri* 9:79–104.

Wajenberg, Arnold and Michael Gorman (1981) "OCLC's Database Conversion: A User's Perspective." *Journal of Library Automation* 14(Sept.):174–189.

Wanninger, P. (1982) "Is the OCLC Database Too Large? A Study of the Effect of Duplicate Records in the OCLC System." *Library Resources and Technical Services* 26(Oct.):353–361.

Wasby, Steven (1978) *The Supreme Court in the Federal Judicial System.* New York, Holt Rinehart Winston.

Washington Library Network (1981) "System Description Introduction: Overview of the WLN Computer System." Olympia, Wash.

Washington State Library. "Five Year Plan." Olympia, Wash.

Weber, Max (1964) *The Theory of Social and Economic Organization.* Ed. by Talcott Parsons. New York, Free Press.

Webster, J. K. and C. L. Warden (1980) "Comparing the Bibliographic Utilities for Special Librarians." *Special Libraries* 71(Dec.):519–522.

Wilensky, Harold (1967) *Organizational Intelligence: Knowledge and Power in Government and Industry.* New York, Basic Books.

———. (1964) "The Professionalization of Everyone?" *American Journal of Sociology* 70(Sept.):137–158.

Wilson, Pauline (1981) "Professionalism Under Attack." *Journal of Academic Librarianship* 7(Nov.):283–290.

Wilson, Patrick (1983) "The Catalog as Access Mechanism: Background and Concepts." *Library Resources and Technical Services* 27(Jan./Mar.):4–17.

———. (1983a) *Second Hand Knowledge: An Inquiry Into Cognitive Authority.* Westport, Conn., Greenwood Press.

The WLN Participant. June 1976–December 1984.

Woods, Richard (1979) "Washington Library Network Computer System." *On-Line Review* 3:297–330.

Yarmolinsky, Adam (1978) "What Future for the Professional in American Society?" *Daedalus* (Winter):159–174.

Zald, Mayer (1976) "On the Social Control of Industries." Unpublished research paper. Vanderbilt University.

———. (1970) *Occupations and Organizations in American Society: The Organization Dominated Man?"* Chicago, Markham Publishing.

Zald, Mayer and Feather D. Hair (1972) "The Social Control of General Hospitals." In *Organization Research on Health Institutions*. Ed. by Basil Georgopoulos. Ann Arbor, University of Michigan, Institute for Social Research, pp. 51–82.

Zola, I. and S. J. Miller (1973) "The Erosion of Medicine From Within." In *The Professions and Their Prospects*. Ed. by Eliot Freidson. Beverly Hills, Sage, pp. 153–172.

Index

152

Index

Fred award, 35

International Standard Bibliographic Description (ISBD), 109
International Federation of Library Associations, 109
Internetwork Quality Control Council (IQCC), 32

Librarians: deprofessionalization, 130–31; professional criteria, 41–44; values, 130
Library assistants, 69–77
Library of Congress (LC): cataloging, 18–19; cataloging rules, 15; MARC, 15, 18, 28, 109–11; quality of cataloging, 15, 29, 33–34; subject headings (LCSH), 15

MARC, 15, 18, 28, 109–11
Master record: Online Computer Library Center (OCLC), 23, 98; Washington Library Network (WLN), 25
Minimal level cataloging, 29, 88–90, 126

Networks: blacklists, 80–81; definition of, 1; documentation, 79–80; error reports, 82, 126; quality, 115; whitelists, 98–99

OCLC. See Online Computer Library Center
Oglebay Institute on Quality Control, 7
Online Computer Library Center (OCLC), 6, 19; authority files, 112; Bibliographic Maintenance Section, 29–30; cataloging levels, 29; data base,
14, 33; documentation, 73; error reporting, 29–33, 84–86; Internetwork Quality Control Council (IQCC), 32; Master record, 23, 98; Pricing Committee, 114; Project Enhance, 35, 92

Peer Groups, of catalogers, 91–94, 97, 100, 106, 126, 128
Pittsburgh Regional Library Center (PRLC), 35
Pricing Committee. See Online Computer Library Center.
Professional organizations, 47–48
Professionals, criteria for, 38–44
Project Enhance. See Online Computer Library Center.

Quality control, 21, 29–36, 92–93; of cataloging, 65–67; Library of Congress, 15, 29, 33–34; networks, 115; Washington Library Network, 35

Research Libraries Group/Research Libraries Information Network (RLG/RLIN), 6, 19, 115; authority files, 112; catalog clusters, 24; error reporting, 83, 85; master record, 24, 98
RLG. See Research Libraries Group
RLIN. See Research Libraries Information Network

San Francisco State University, 6, 87, 95
San Jose State University, 6, 86
Social control, 48–49, 79, 126
Sonoma State University, 6, 86

About the Author

RUTH HAFTER is the Director of the Ruben Salazar Library of Sonoma State University.

WITHDRAWN
FROM STOCK